Never Pay Retail Again

D0974607

Never Pay Retail Again

Shop Smart, Spend Less, and Look Your Best Ever

DAISY LEWELLYN

G

Gallery Books

New York   London   Toronto   Sydney

GALLERY BOOKS

A Division of Simon & Schuster, Inc.
1230 Avenue of the Americas
New York, NY 10020

First Gallery Books trade paperback edition May 2010

GALLERY BOOKS and colophon are trademarks of Simon & Schuster, Inc.

For information about special discounts for bulk purchases, please contact
Simon & Schuster Special Sales at 1-866-506-1949 or business@simonandschuster.com.

The Simon & Schuster Speakers Bureau can bring authors to your live event. For
more information or to book an event contact the Simon & Schuster Speakers Bureau
at 1-866-248-3049 or visit our website at www.simonspeakers.com.

Designed by Dana Sloan

Manufactured in the United States of America

10   9   8   7   6   5   4   3   2   1

Library of Congress Cataloging-in-Publication Data

Lewellyn, Daisy.
    Never pay retail again : shop smart, spend less, and look your best ever / by Daisy
Lewellyn.
        p. cm.
1. Clothing and dress.   2. Shopping.   I. Title.
    TT507.L463 2010
    746.9'20681—dc22

                                                                                    2009046581

ISBN 978-1-4391-6735-9
ISBN 978-1-4391-6736-6 (ebook)

To the two original Bargain Babes,

Granny and Nana, xo Miss Priss

Contents

Contents

Introduction

Fashion is in my genes. A fourth-generation seamstress, I was born into a family of fashion lovers. If my Granny, Mildred McGill, had ten bucks, she would sew an amazing dress for herself *and* one for her sister—and each would look as if they were worth hundreds of dollars. My late Nana, Louisia Samm, lived to be nearly eighty and was still sporting stacked heels and fabulously exquisite hats until her final days. Both women passed on a secret to me that has a special place in my heart: you don't have to spend a lot to achieve your best personal style.

We've always been a fashion-forward family. My sister wore a lime green leather pencil skirt and matching bustier to her prom's after-party in 1990 and passed down her Guess jeans obsession to me (we would take trips to Tijuana for deals at the Guess outlet). At just two years old, my niece T'sai stumbled around the house in my silver sequined, high-heeled mules. And my niece Assata loves to dress "fancy." Like I said, I'm surrounded by full-fledged fashion girls.

I always knew I was destined for a career in fashion. My junior year at Howard University, I did an exchange program at New York City's Fashion Institute of Technology to study accessories design. I also interned at *Honey Magazine*, which was beyond cool at the time. I instantly fell in love with the world of fashion and craved every bit of it. After graduation, my very first job was back in Manhattan at *InStyle* magazine working under fashion legend Sydne Bolden, who taught me the ins and outs of making it in the business. I was living out my most glamorous dream. Only one minor issue . . . my reality was a $23,000 salary before taxes. I quickly learned that a clothing allowance could not equal your entire paycheck. It was time to be resourceful. My sample sale education and designer-duds-for-less passion took off. I soon gained notoriety as an expert on turning runway looks into affordable fashion. The matriarchs of my family were right: It *is* fun and smart to stand apart from the crowd as a true fashion girl while secretly smiling about all the money you've saved.

Between living in Los Angeles and New York, and going to Howard University in Washington, DC, and traveling everywhere from Texas for family reunions to the Midwest for work, I am always faced with compassion and frustration. Why? Because I hear the same falsehood from women: if you don't live in a big city, there is nowhere for you to shop. *Huh?!* That is so *not true,* but it seems far too many women still feel this way, despite the abundance of online shopping sites. Then there is the biggie, the humdinger that seems to always circulate on playdate park benches and checkout line chitchat: *Clothes are just too expensive these days. I don't have the money or time to get all dressed up and I really cannot afford the fancy stores.* Oh, my stars, I have to stop myself from shaking the clipped coupons out of these ladies I hear spew such nonsense. And then there are the women who are pretty well versed in the lower-priced shopping resources but really don't know how to spend twenty dollars to get an item worth two hundred dollars and spend way too much money on the absolute *wrong* things.

I can't wait to share my editing abilities so that you too can shop smart and save bundles of cash! This book is designed for women who want to look like a million bucks but also want to save a pretty penny. Cue the lights and enter from stage left: the Bargain Babe. Consider me your Bargain Babe Style Coach. *Never Pay Retail Again* is your guide, resource, and how-to for all things bargain and discount—and sometimes even free. Get ready to indulge in the stylish delights of fashion and beauty without massive credit card debt, a trust fund, or a Gucci bag as your pillow after you find yourself homeless. You can shop and eat, shop and put the kids through college, shop and do a really smart thing—save. It's *très* chic to be stylish and financially smart. And it's really possible without feeling like you are confined in a fun-free zone. I love Target for their diffusion lines, I'm obsessed with Bergdorf's for their amazing shoe sales, and I never met a T.J. Maxx that I didn't adore. My goal is for every girl to tap into her inner Bargain Babe.

This means looking your best with all of your purchases, from the "running errands" look to the after-five cocktail number. But instead of bulk and quantity, you will be inspired to focus on wearability for your lifestyle, flattering silhouettes, and chic styles. A large wardrobe does not necessarily equal your best-looking wardrobe. When you purchase pieces that make you look your best, you will feel your best. I'm offering the freedom to wear the styles and brands that you love—even those that you have always dreamed of wearing but thought you could never afford.

Shopaholics reformed into Bargain Babes need to milk this moment for all it's worth. This is the time to boast and brag about all things bargain, markdown, and clearance. Even our beautiful First Lady, Michelle Obama, is a self-proclaimed Bargain Babe and does not mind sharing her love for a deal (the White House has never seen so much J.Crew candy-colored goodness!). Websites like InStyle .com, People.com, and StyleBakery.com serve up yummy bargains and styles seen on celebs on a pretty platter. You can now find out what Beyoncé wore to the airport, to the Grammys, or even to Starbucks. Not to mention that they provide the exact label *and* a cheaper replica. So many depressed lovelies are now just a click away from fashion restoration and redemption.

Never Pay Retail Again is the long-awaited wake-up call of creative inspiration, timeless tips, and fashion fantasies.

Long live the Bargain Babe!

Inspired Style

UNLEASH YOUR TRUE FASHION PERSONALITY

You are just steps away from becoming a lifelong Bargain Babe. But before you brag about your savings to the girls, we need to tackle one essential step: identifying your personal style. It's your fashion compass, the thing that keeps you on course when confronted with endless options. It's what tells you a beautiful flowy bohemian printed dress is right for you, while that belted shirtdress has your best friend's name all over it. Without having a sense of personal style, shopping will overwhelm you, and you'll find yourself with a closet filled with clothes but nothing to wear. When you aren't confident in your own vision, you wind up with purchases simply because (1) they were on sale, (2) your sister thought you looked adorable in them, or (3) a salesperson did some fast commission-boosting talking. None of those reasons are good for your style or your wallet.

You might be looking to develop your personal style—which we'll do in the next couple of chapters—but you have an intuitive sense of what you like and don't like. You aren't going to start wearing leopard prints and miniskirts all of a sudden when you've gravitated to tailored suits your whole life. The point is, a little self-knowledge can lead to a whole lot of shopping as you learn which stores, websites, styles, and designers work for *you*.

Find Your Style Personality

From shopping with countless women, I've discovered that many fall into at least one of the major categories below. Which description best matches your style personality? You may be a combination of two or three. Don't worry, you're not a style schizo. These are guidelines to get you thinking about your look so that when that oversize ruffled pirate shirt by a top designer that wouldn't even look good on Heidi Klum has been marked down from a thousand dollars to a hundred dollars, you can walk away with confidence.

THE CLASSIC GIRL

You consider "trend" a dirty word. You love a crisp white shirt, a well-cut trench, and a wonderfully tailored shift dress in midnight black. Audrey Hepburn is your style icon.

THE BOHEMIAN BABE

You gravitate toward fabrics that have fluidity and ease and hate anything too tailored. The sixties style icon Talitha Getty is your fairy godmother.

THE TREND-DRIVEN DIVA

You love being current with the latest trends and styles. Your friends come to you to ask what's in this season. *Vogue* and *Elle* magazines are your style bibles.

THE POSH PRINCESS

Your style is very pulled together and chic. You're a fan of structured silhouettes and outfits that have a precise theme. Think Blair Waldorf in *Gossip Girl*.

THE COLOR-IS-MY-MIDDLE-NAME CUTIE

You're not afraid to tango with tangerine or salsa with saffron. A love for color ignites your mood. You light up the darkest rooms. Michelle Obama's fearless choices inspire you.

THE NOIR-IS-THE-NEW-BLACK BETTY

Never mind what the magazines do or don't say, black is the new black in your book. It's your go-to hue no matter the season or the state. You prefer to look like a New Yorker even if you're strolling the sands of Malibu.

THE FEMININE FRILLY

You embrace your girly side with sweet details like lace, ruffles, and bows. The color pink reigns supreme. Think Mariah Carey with her love of sparkles and butterflies.

THE SEXY SEDUCTRESS

You like to stir up a little trouble by wearing form-fitting fabrics and showing a little more skin than the average gal. Salma Hayek and Beyoncé are your style icons.

THE VINTAGE VIXEN

You love making a piece from another era look modern and fresh, preferring one-of-a-kind vintage items to off-the-rack ready-to-wear. You love watching celebrity stylist Rachel Zoe hunt for treasures, and you think Sienna Miller has a killer eye.

THE SPORTY SPICE

Sneakers and cargo pants are your idea of wardrobe staples. You look for plenty of flexibility and room for movement in your clothes. Venus and Serena—on the court—are your role models.

Lifestyle

You may envision yourself as a Posh Princess, but you spend all day taking care of two very messy toddlers. Or you are a Sporty Spice at heart but run a large corporation where you are expected to wear serious suits every day. While it's great to have fantasies and desires, you also need to realistically tailor your look to your lifestyle. This will ensure you don't waste money on clothes that are for a totally different person's life. Ask yourself the following questions to get thinking about the clothes that will really suit you.

WHAT ARE MY WEEKENDS LIKE?

Your weekends might involve a lot of socializing and family activities. One huge style myth is that casual or comfortable means schleppy. The truth is, casual has never looked so good. There are stylish jackets in comfy sweatshirt material and flattering silhouettes, not to mention a million cute pairs of jeans. There are also dresses that are so comfy you feel like you're in a nightgown.

WHAT ARE MY ROLES?

Are you a mom to mini future NFL players whose hugs come with dirt and grass stains? Shout it out and dress in pieces that can easily be washed. Are you an assistant? Dress for the position that you want, not the position you have. Are you a dog walker? There are fabulous sneaker options (supermodel Veronica Webb suggests Puma and Tiger). No matter what your role or title, there are stylish options to suit your lifestyle.

WHERE DO I LIVE, AND WHAT IS THE WEATHER LIKE?

Weather and region play huge roles in your lifestyle. If you don't like the overall personal style of the region that you live in, dare to be different and wear what suits you. If you are in a cold climate, think about buying beautiful pieces that keep you warm and make you feel good: elbow-length, bold-colored gloves, wool newsboy hats, chunky colorful knit sweaters, knit dresses, fur- or wool-lined leather boots, thick textured tights—oh, the list just goes on and on.

WHAT AM I ALWAYS DOING?

It seems like an obvious question, but take a few minutes to think about it. Are you always running late with no time to do your hair? Stock up on stylish hat options like fedoras instead of the mom-jean equivalent for heads—baseball caps. If you catch public transportation, go for stylish flats instead of frumpy sneakers.

WHAT ARE MY GOALS AND WISHES?

This is a perfect time to open the door to trying new experiences. If you want to start hosting parties or try salsa dancing, make a mental note when shopping. Be open to purchasing pieces that are not a part of your daily routine but will become a part of your expanded lifestyle.

SHOP TALK WITH . . . **Amy Elisa Keith,**

People magazine writer

"Casual doesn't mean sloppy. You can still be comfy and casual while looking polished. Wear a crisp white tank top or a new white V-neck shirt with jeans, and throw on some hoop earrings with it and a great pair of flat sandals. If you're wearing baggy sweats, stay away from a baggy shirt. If you're wearing sneakers, wear a bit of makeup and accessorize."

Get Inspired to Shop!

Inspiration allows your personal style to continuously evolve. And it can come from nearly anywhere. Designers base their collections on inspirations that range from the color and texture of their favorite kitchen spice to where they went on their summer vacations. It's that free and spontaneous; there are no rules! Inspiration can take your attitude about getting dressed from depressing to delightful.

How will evolving your style help you become a better shopper? Well, first of all, this is supposed to be fun. So the more you can experience fashion as an exciting way to express yourself, and not as some preconceived notion of how you should look, the more you'll enjoy your clothes. But digging yourself out of a fashion rut (yes, I'm talking to those of you who have the same dress in every color of blah), or opening up to wider possibilities that still fit your general style, will give you many more options when you hit the stores in search of bargains. If you know how to play with pieces, you'll be able to incorporate lots of hidden gems passed over by the ordinary shopper.

Now, some may think that you have to live a glamorous life filled with champagne days and diamond nights in order to be inspired. But it does not matter if you live in Ibiza or Idaho: it's all about tapping into whatever sources give you a rush. Start by heading to your local bookstore or newsstand. Peruse fashion magazines, lifestyle books, catalogs, and party planning books—they're all full of fabulous, inspiration-laden photos. Think of a woman whose style you really admire, whether she's a celebrity or your next-door neighbor. Take note of the confidence that she exudes. Maybe she wears full skirts or boasts bold-colored tops or always has freshly blown out hair. Take particular note of women who share similar traits to your own, like hair or skin color. If you're blond and have a blond coworker who always looks great in nude and cream, try the same. Always be on the lookout for well-dressed women who share your body shape, then analyze their look. Maybe you have a petite frame like Eva Longoria Parker. Find inspiration in her ability to always look amazing, whether at a basketball game or on the red carpet, and apply it to *your* wardrobe. When I style segments for television, women always say, "Hmm, I would never have thought to do that!" Sometimes the courage to try something new comes only after you've seen it done successfully on someone else. On the other hand, it's just as important to observe another person's *mistakes* to prevent your own personal fashion disaster.

Get in the Mood

Another way to visualize a more stylish you is to create your very own mood board. It's a great visual reminder of your goal. What exactly *is* a mood board? It's a personal collection of images, fabric swatches, photos, postcards, pages torn from magazines, and anything else that inspires you. Walk into any fashion designer's office, and you'll find mood boards galore. Fashion editors and stylists also create mood boards to generate looks for their magazine pages or clients. Inspiration is fashion's life-blood—I can't stress that enough. Without inspiration, the fashion industry would not exist. To look your best, you need to tap into the same process.

The PTA moms seem to have scrapbooking covered, so now it's time for us fashion girls to have a little project. Your next assignment is to put together a mood board with all of your life and wardrobe inspirations. Think of it as the most fashionable arts and crafts project that you will ever make.

Creating Your Mood Board

Making a mood board is lots of fun—and even somewhat therapeutic. It allows you to get in touch with your inner passions and the alter ego (hello, inner showgirl!) you're afraid to unlock.

Begin by clipping, collecting, and stashing any image or material that catches your eye—you can edit down later. Snag a sharp pair of scissors (or pinking shears for a pretty zigzag border effect) and a box of push pins. Assemble the mood board on a canvas of your choice. An easy option is a large corkboard that you can pick up at any office supply store. Or, if you want to be *très* chic, try using a thrift store painting with a cool vintage frame and just cover the picture with your materials.

If you are a techie and prefer smooth fingertips to paper cuts, you can create a virtual mood board. Compile images from online, or even scan your materials. After saving, cut and paste them all into one document, sizing and arranging to suit your liking. You can print the finished product or even make it your screen saver!

Regardless of the format, make sure that you spend a little quality time looking over your mood board, even if it's just a few seconds every day. By constantly checking your gallery of inspiration, you will effortlessly become your own best fashion editor. Your office, closet, or near your bedroom mirror are great places to keep your board. And you should create a new mood board at least twice a year, just before spring and then again for fall. A few items may remain constant—a photo of your style icon, perhaps—but it's only natural for your mood and needs to change with the weather. For instance, an image of a great Fendi fur coat might be swapped for a shot of your favorite summer *Miami, here I come* thong sandals.

MOOD BOARD MATERIALS

- Tear sheets from magazines, catalogs, and newspapers
- Portrait of you looking your best (gotta have something to top, right?!)
- Photos of style muses (a couple of my personal favorites are Diana Ross and Jackie O, but most people are not as dramatic as I am!)
- Pictures of inspiring family members
- Favorite designer looks
- Pictures of items that you plan on style stalking until you get your hands on them
- Favorite colors and prints displayed on ribbons, fabric swatches, paint swatch cards, or home decor images
- Heartfelt items (a special brooch that you wore on a memorable occasion, the button that fell off your coat the night you met your husband). Not everyone puts this kind of thing on their mood board, but I'm a fanatic for romantic memories
- Life mantras and mottos—whether they're from Jesus, your late grandpa, or your favorite poet, inspirational quotes and words can really tie together your mood board

Covered in glue, surrounded by stacks of your favorite magazines or dreamily staring at a picture of your fantasy boots, you are getting your fashion juices flowing. Now let's move on to real materials. I'm talking cashmere, silk, leather . . . you know, clothes. Fired up by inspiration and grounded with a vision of your personal style, you are ready to get into the nitty-gritty of building the perfect wardrobe.

Shopping 2 Planner

Stepping into a posh boutique, a department store, or a tempting designer sample sale without a plan of action is like walking into a PETA rally wearing a cognac fox fur coat and leather thigh-high boots. In other words, it's a fashion *don't!* Unless you want to end up with a pair of six-inch-heeled designer pumps that are painful to stand in, never mind walk in, you *must* do some prep work before you brave that Bergdorf shoe sale. And it's not just the high-ticket items that you have to plan for—there's no point in buying a pile of twenty-buck cheapie flats if you have to spend thirty bucks on ointment for the nasty blisters they give you.

Devising a shopping strategy in advance is the best way to maximize purchases using minimal cash. It will help you know what you are doing. You'll be rewarded with great clothes and stellar shopping stories to share with the gals in the salon afterward. But before you can start showing off, you have to understand a key factor to shopping smart: you. What kind of shopper are you? What are your weaknesses and strengths? What kind of clothes fit you best? Are you into trends, classics, or a little bit of both? Last, you'll figure out exactly what items you need to build the perfect wardrobe so you can shop with a plan.

What Kind of Shopper Are You?

If you want to shop smart, spend less, and look your best ever, you are going to have to take a few sips of strong brisk Honest Tea. What's your shopping track record? Do you buy only black clothes? Own forty-seven pairs of sandals and not a single pair of office-ready pumps? Or are you the girl who buys tons of great pieces—except they're better suited to pretty much any body type but your own?

One of the toughest parts of savvy shopping is the honesty required to do it well. Anyone can shop: walk into a store, pick out an item, give the clerk some cash or a credit card, and you have officially shopped. But becoming a shopping *expert* requires more than just an AmEx and a mall directory. In order to be a truly great shopper, you have to be honest about your personal style, lifestyle, budget, fears, and joys.

The first step in getting your shopping license is to identify what kind of shopper you are. From my experience shopping with tons of women, I've discovered six major categories: Impulse, Emotional, Alter Ego, Cowardly Lion, Dollars and No Sense, and Smart. Let's see which hits closest to home for you. And don't be surprised or feel silly if more than one category applies, because different days can definitely bring out alternate or even dual shopping personalities.

THE IMPULSE SHOPPER

You see something you love, you buy it. Your mind rationalizes, "I saw this in a magazine—buy it!" And then there's the ever popular "It's Prada and it's my size—buy it!" You shop on a whim, without a plan or a purpose, ending up with a closet full of marked-down fur even if you live in the middle of sun-scorched Arizona. If you're bothered by the nagging question of *why* you're buying yet another pair of mink earmuffs, the answer is usually "Why not!? Now leave me alone and pass the matching hat!"

THE EMOTIONAL SHOPPER

You have a great day at work, so you celebrate with a cupcake and a shopping spree. Or you're devastated by a breakup, so you drown your sorrows in shopping bags and a parmesan mall pretzel. Even when you're just bored, you head for the mall. You don't shop because you desire a specific item; you shop because you're looking for comfort and fulfillment within the confines of a boutique. Emotions come and go, but purchases have a way of being permanent. You don't need a couch and a shrink to figure this out. Some call it retail therapy . . . I call it a setup for an overcrowded closet full of "What the heck was I thinking?"

THE ALTER EGO SHOPPER

Everything you buy looks absolutely fantastic, darling! There's only one issue: it looks great on someone else. Perhaps you have a few more curves than the average gal, but for some reason all of your pieces are better suited for a lean lanky lady. Or you're the slim girl with an athletic build, but all of your clothes would look better on someone with a Beyoncé-liscious hourglass shape. The alter ego shopper gets excited when something looks cute on the hanger, regardless of the way it looks on her body.

THE COWARDLY LION SHOPPER

You've got your look and you're sticking to it! In fact, you've been attached to this safety zone look ever since your now adult daughter was riding a Big Wheel. Safe and predictable—at work or at play—that's you. Between the multiple drab separates and the yawn-inducing colors, your closet looks like a storage room for hotel employees' uniforms, and I'm not talking a swanky boutique hotel. In your life, clothes are utilitarian, without an ounce of excitement or fun. What are you hiding from? Face it, you're bored with your wardrobe and it's bored with you. Instead of expressing yourself, you're stuck in a navy blue style rut.

THE DOLLARS AND NO SENSE SHOPPER

You set out to buy a pair of ballet flats to wear with the kids on the weekends, and you come home with six-inch fire-engine red peep-toe heels that cost the equivalent of a small country's GDP—*again*. You somehow always spend too much money on purchases that you later regret, and not enough money on the items you know you really need. You passed basic arithmetic in fifth grade, so it can't be a math issue. Buyer's remorse is such a bummer.

THE SMART SHOPPER

You know what looks great on your body type, and you're loyal and dedicated to your most flattering silhouettes. You are very clear on the needs of your lifestyle and focus on what will have the strongest shelf life in your wardrobe. You explore trends that work specifically for you, not just ones that look great on a model. And perhaps most important, you consider what you've already got in your closet before you plunk down your hard-earned cash.

If you selected any of the categories above—even the Smart Shopper—read on for tips to improve your shopping habits and debut a more fabulous you. Even savvy shoppers will learn something new and inspiring.

SHOP TALK WITH . . . **Julee Wilson, fashion editor of *Real Simple* magazine**

"If you don't love it, put it down. If it doesn't fit now, it never will. If you put something on and start dancing in the mirror, it's a winner!"

Wardrobe Building

Establishing a well-rounded wardrobe is essential to bringing ease and a sense of order into your daily routine. Wardrobe building helps you conquer that infamous task every woman struggles with: choosing what to wear every day. Say you love cashmere turtlenecks. Splendid, so do I! But if you have a closet full of cashmere snugglies in every color from raspberry to kelly green and not a skirt, pant, dress, or earring in sight, there's a problem with your fashion pendulum! What are you going to wear with all your beautiful sweaters? The same pair of black pants over and over again?

Wardrobe building is the gradual process of creating a complete collection of apparel and accessories that suit your specific fashion needs. Build your wardrobe well and you'll never be stuck in the "I have nothing to wear" twilight zone. Now, don't feel like you have to go out and buy every single missing item on the list in one weekend. That would be pretty exhausting on your pockets, even with great deals on everything. It will take time, but it's an extremely rewarding undertaking. When you're done, you'll be fashionably prepared for absolutely every occasion that comes your way for years, even decades, to come. It's all about shopping smart with a true Bargain Babe mentality of "best quality, best price," all while building a more efficient balanced wardrobe.

There are three questions to ask yourself when wardrobe building:

1. What do I have?
2. What do I need?
3. What do I want?

WHAT DO I HAVE?

First, observe. Take a free Saturday and really assess your closet and any packed-away clothes, including the boxes in the garage and the items buried at the back of the coat closet. When you look over the inventory, are you excited to see your pieces, or do you have an overwhelming desire to take a nap? Think about the message your clothes give. For instance, take your shoes. If a person didn't know you, would they observe your footwear and think you were a trendy teenager, a middle-aged housewife, an elementary school teacher, or a conservative matron? Decide if the message your clothes and accessories are sending is the message that represents your true personality and lifestyle.

How Do I Really Look?

Invite a fashionable and honest friend over to walk you through your wardrobe-building steps. Sometimes we look at our wardrobes so much that we get tunnel vision—it's hard to see what our clothes actually look like. A trusted friend's eye will always bring a fresh outlook to your wardrobe. And though a true friend would be willing to devote time to helping you wardrobe build without any strings attached, it's always nice to serve something fruity to drink and offer savory snacks to keep your pal focused and happy.

WHAT DO I NEED?

Every closet should be balanced and well rounded. Don't be like the lonely singleton who leaves the grocery store with nothing but mac 'n' cheese, a pint of Rum Raisin, and a six-pack of Coke. Without any veggies, fruits, or whole grains to balance out a meal, how can you expect to look and feel healthy? Establishing your needs in advance allows you to avoid buying too much of the same thing or not enough of the right thing. Always be aware of and open to purchasing what you need, not just what you want. If your prized jean collection belongs in a fashion museum but you don't have any great tops to snazz them up for a night out on the town, it's time to cut back on True Religion and Hanes tank tops and pick up some nicer blouses to dress up your impressive denim. And don't feel held back by the seasons. If you stumble upon a great deal on boots in midsummer and you know you'll really, really need (and love) them for fall, go ahead and buy them to bring out when the sunshine goes on hiatus. It will be like having Christmas early when you pull them out in October.

WHAT DO I WANT?

This is the question most women ask themselves when shopping. Every season you should have a mental "What I Want List" (I like to write it down and then check items off as I acquire my prizes—it's very satisfying!). Once you establish what you really want, you'll be destined for a high success rate while shopping. You can watch items online and in stores, alert the sales girls to the faves that will fit your budget much nicer once they go on sale, and save up in advance for what needs to come home to your closet. If you have a clear idea of what you want and don't just decide you want everything you see while you are at the department store, you'll be transformed into a shopping pro!

I will never forget the day I purchased a pair of chocolate brown crocodile Manolo Blahnik pumps for two hundred dollars. The beauty director at *Glamour*, where I was working at the time, was selling them during my towering shoe obsession phase (which has not left me since). I *really really really* wanted them. And though I didn't make much money at the time, I snagged them quicker than you can say "investment buy" because (1) they were two hundred dollars and real crocodile!! and (2) they were a classic shape and style created by one of the industry's finest shoe designers. I knew they would never lose their status as a timeless classic. It was like welcoming a famous chef into your kitchen; you are guaranteed to have a good meal. Mr. Manolo always serves up a great-quality shoe. I figured I could pass them on to my daughter. The daughter still has not been born, but the pumps remain in tip-top shape.

Be selective in deciding what you want. Base your decisions on what you already have and in what direction your style is going. For example, say you need a new coat and you want to move in a more tailored, elegant direction. Resolve to buy the best tailored trench or sleek coat you can get your hands on. May I suggest searching Burlington Coat Factory, Loehmann's, Filene's Basement, Marshalls, Century 21, and T.J. Maxx for fabulous designer options for less? Decide how much you want to spend on items in advance, and once you've set a price limit, stick to it. And, finally, buy only things that will tickle your fancy for longer than two months. Items that have a longer shelf life than a season are always better choices to bring home to the fashion family in your closet. Applying self-control and a laser beam focus translates into shopping success!

SHOP TALK WITH . . . **Warren Satchell,**
senior merchant for specialty retailers

"It's all about shopping like the Europeans. Buy five to ten key statement pieces that are interchangeable, and the rest of your apparel and shoes are just fill-ins that complement those five to ten key pieces."

Inside the Ideal Wardrobe

Fashion and style are about self-expression, as I have said. But as with any incredible art form, there are a few universal rules one must follow. After you assess your current clothing situation, figure out the holes, and then stoke your fantasies, you'll be ready to dive into the next phase of your shopping quest. However, before you take a single step toward your new look, let's familiarize ourselves with the essential building blocks to any great wardrobe.

TIMELESS ESSENTIALS

Pieces commonly referred to as "classics" provide a stable foundation upon which you can easily build a strong wardrobe. These items extend the overall shelf life of your wardrobe and can easily transition from season to season, even year to year, because they don't go out of style. They're also great for mixing with trendier pieces to create a more balanced, wearable look.

One of the biggest fashion myths is that classic items can't have any personality . . . they're just basic and boring and exist purely for pairing with trendy pieces. Wrong! While classics are always fun to pair up with other kinds of pieces, they should not exude *yaaaaaawn* and *boooring* on their own. They should be timeless and chic, and accommodate your personal style and taste. Yes, every woman should own a great white shirt, but yours may be an Anne Fontaine with a ruffled neck, and your sister's may be from Nordstrom with French cuffs and crystal buttons. Essentials, like a tailored cashmere coat or a pencil skirt, are wonderful options for investment pieces. Since they will be able to easily transition from year to year, it's best to buy quality items that will last with proper TLC and maintenance rather than stock up on ten white collared shirts that look like uniforms.

SIGNATURE DEFINERS

Signature style is one of my favorite parts of fashion; it's really what a person becomes known for, whether in the pages of glossy gossip mags or just among your girlfriends. Think Coco Chanel and her pearls, Michelle Obama and her belted cardigans, *Vogue*'s Anna Wintour and her razored bob and fierce sunglasses. Because it focuses your wardrobe, honing your signature style is a wonderful way to look pulled together and sharp without spending money on lots of clothes and accessories.

Every woman should tap into her signature style. You will appear polished and confident if you just focus, focus, focus! It's a sort of a special, secret pass to sneak your style passions through repeat offender—dom. It can define you and what you love, instead of making you appear as if you have nothing else to wear. Remember cashmere turtleneck girl from a few pages ago? Give that girl a beautiful blazer, a sick pump, and a chic pencil skirt, and those turtlenecks go from yawn to yes! My signature style includes dresses, lots of color, belted trench coats, platform shoes, and hoop earrings—that's pretty much my uniform. I don't care what the season's trend reports say is a must-have or a must-stash; these are my babies, and I love to mix and match colors and textures so my style looks focused, fresh, and current.

It's important to allow your style to be defined by what you love, before allowing someone else to tell you what to love. Let magazines and celebrity styles inspire you (remember your mood board!) and get your wheels turning, not define what you have to look like. Your signature style can be simple and understated, or over-the-top and dramatic. It's your choice, as long as you can claim it to be yours and only yours. Own it!

FASHION ICONS' SIGNATURE STYLE

Anna Wintour	Razored bob and oversize shades
Karl Lagerfeld	Collared white shirts and skinny black blazers
André Leon Talley	Over-the-top capes
Audrey Hepburn	Cigarette pants and ballet flats
Michelle Obama	Belted cardis and color, color, color!
Jennifer Aniston	All-American Beauty meets Girl Next Door in denim and cotton
Sienna Miller	Hippie-chic hats paired with hipster essentials
Kate Hudson	Flowing pieces, just like mama Goldie
Rihanna	Fierce tailored jackets and skinny jeans with stacked heels

CLOSET SOCIALITES

It is important to buy what I call social items. At work, on the weekends, on vacation, or wherever, they look right at home in most situations and with most outfits. A great pair of nude flat sandals can work with colored pieces, black and white, and even printed looks. A perfect-fitting pair of dark denim jeans can be dressed down with a white tank or ready for a night on the town with a sexy playful blouse. Building your wardrobe with versatile pieces is an excellent way to get your full money's worth. And surprise, surprise, the social item does not always have to be something in black or neutral. For example, solid-colored pastel cardigans work with black, white, nude, and more, just as well as a black cardigan does.

SHOES AND BAGS

A common mistake that women make is overlooking their shoes and bags. While shoes are there to cover your feet, and bags are the best for loading up coupons and cash, they can also be immediate confidence boosters. Try carrying a bright bold bag for a week, and notice the difference in responses from complete strangers. Shoes and bags can bring life to even the simplest getup. How do you think celebrities manage to look great going to the gym with a messy ponytail? Check out their statement bag. Or what about the hot paparazzi shots of Eva Longoria Parker and Beyoncé at basketball games with their beaus? They will have on jeans, a smile, and a killer pair of heels. Now, I am not insisting that you sport your marked-down Jimmy Choo pumps to little Billy's flag football game—just up the shoe style ante by embracing quality.

UNDER IT ALL

Proper-fitting undergarments are key! Your base and foundation are important to secure before you layer clothes on top. If you have a variety of great panties, bras, and shapewear, all your clothes will fit their absolute best. Too-tight undergarments can make you look heavier, and nobody likes that! Remember, if everyone is busy looking at your highly visible, wretched panty lines, they will never be able to appreciate the wonderful skirt or jeans you're sporting.

When it comes to bras, embrace variety, because one style will not work for everything in your closet. You definitely need a few workhorse bras for everyday, but I'm also a firm believer that all women should own at least one piece of beautiful lingerie—no matter your relationship status. You'll radiate feelings of sexiness, even if no one but you knows what's underneath.

Don't mistake your undergarments for outergarments. Let's leave a little mystery to others. A textured lace bra is not acceptable worn with a thin T-shirt, even if it is La Perla. But don't go crying into your scalloped cups, ladies. La Perla lace is perfect under a more structured blouse where it won't show through. Especially when you were smart enough to snag marked-down pieces at the La Perla outlet.

On a more functional note, a good hosiery wardrobe of opaque tights is a must-have in my world. They are a big lifesaver for taking peep toe shoes from summer to fall. Go for opaque tights in slimming dark neutrals like black, navy, and gray—they are a great updated alternative to sheer hosiery.

SHOP TALK WITH . . . **Diana Oberlander,**
celebrity stylist

"Never forget the proper underclothes and undergarments. Try wearing silk slips underneath dresses and skirts to smooth out the body."

PUT A RING ON IT

Jewelry is definitely something you will collect year after year until . . . well, really, until you are pushing up daisies! Jewelry is something a woman acquires all her life and can pass down from generation to generation. Birthday gifts from Dad, pieces from your dear grandma, and special finds that you score at estate sales from someone else's grandmother are wonderful to add to your collection. It's nice to have a mix of real jewelry—there's nothing wrong with buying it for yourself, by the way—and fabulous costume pieces.

SHOP TALK WITH . . . Rajni Jacques-Dowd, fashion editor of *Nylon* magazine

"I am a very basic dresser. I like my accessories to speak for themselves. And always stock up on the basics—pencil skirts, jeans, a good tube dress, etc. As long as you have those things, you can dress it up or down with great accessories."

The Importance of Fit

The only way to figure out what fits best on you is to try all kinds of shapes and silhouettes. Check yourself out in a three-way mirror. Once you get past the instant shock, you will be glad you took the courageous leap. It shows you the complete picture others see. You may have worn capris all your life, but in reality they might make your legs look shorter and wider because of the cropped length.

GET FIT

When trying on clothes and accessories (yes, there are rules for stuff like bags and jewelry too!), consider these specific areas to ensure a perfect fit.

Pants and Shorts

If they pull, bunch, or pucker near the inner thigh or seat area, try the next size up. Also pay attention to length. The pants should be floor length and expose the front of your shoe only. Mini shorts should not expose the bottom of your bum, and Bermuda shorts should cut off at the slimmest part of your thigh, usually an inch above the knee.

Skirts and Dresses

Calf-length hems usually make you look larger on the bottom. Showing a little or a lot of knee is a much better option.

Tops

A flattering neckline depends a lot on the fullness and shape of your face, the style of your hair, and the size of your bust. Try on a variety of styles—including scoop necks, V-necks, and boatnecks—to find the styles that make your neck look slimmest. For most everyone, exposing your décolleté is very flattering. When it comes to sleeves, women with fuller arms should shy away from cap sleeves or those that cut right at the widest part of the arm. Go all the way—either sleeveless or wrist length. Be mindful of the width of your straps. Spaghetti straps on broad shoulders may get lost. Opt for a fuller width to balance out the upper body. The opposite is true if you have a small upper body.

Shoes

If you are worried about the dreaded cankles—thick-looking ankles—go for sandals without an ankle strap and pointed-toe pumps. Stay away from booties that cut off at the ankle.

Bags

Go for a bag that balances out your frame, and carry it in places that are universally flattering, like on your wrist or in your hand. Wearing your purse across your chest may not be the best place if you have a fuller bust or larger tummy. If you have full arms, a small short-strapped purse will make them larger—especially if you carry it directly under your arm. If you are really petite and love a large bag but are worried about drowning in leather, choose a smaller version of the bag, since many bags have at least two size options in any given style.

Jewelry

Make sure that the dimensions of your jewelry work with your frame. If you are petite, don't weigh yourself down with an excessive amount of pieces. On the other hand, don't allow your size or body weight to drown out your accessories, like wearing a tight choker on a full neck or thin stackable rings on full fingers.

The way pieces are cut—how long and how short, how tight and how loose—is the basis of assessing fit. Showing your knees can make such a difference. A skirt that hits about an inch above the knee is so much more flattering than a skirt that hits at the calf or just above the ankle. Maybe you have fuller thighs and feel very self-conscious about them. Instead of wearing pantsuits to work, why not consider A-line skirt suits to hide your problem areas and accent your shapely calves?

Once you decide on what fits you best, stick to it. It can be tough doing the fit check, but it's better to figure out what works before you make a purchase or wear it out in public. If you know pencil skirts and single-breasted blazers flatter you best, always be on the lookout for them in different colors and textures. If something makes you feel larger than you really are, think about *why* it does and how you can address the issue. You may need to opt for a completely different style altogether, or make a minor adjustment to sidestep the problem.

The all-time solution for making pieces that *almost* fit really work is a great tailor. You may be a classic size eight in Gap jeans but are always belting the waist so tight you feel your small intestine shift. Enlisting a tailor to put a few darts and seams in the waist will make you feel like you are wearing jeans custom designed for your body alone, because, well, they pretty much are. Tailors are not limited to making things smaller. Letting out a seam or two can be so forgiving, you might forget all about counting calories.

Fit does not generally change with trends or seasons. Be loyal to what works for you, but don't be loyal to a number size. Designers and stores all cut their clothes differently. You may be a six in one chain store brand, and an eight or ten with a European designer. Who cares? Try your normal size, and then a size or two up or down if needed. It's better to look good in your clothes than to freak out about the number on the tag.

Best Stores for Your Body

Petite

Many women think petite has to mean a smaller size, but "petite" comes in every size from a two to a fourteen. The clothes are cut for women with shorter arms and legs. The best stores for petites are:

(continued)

- Ann Taylor
- Gap
- Banana Republic
- Macy's
- Forever 21

Curvy

No need to starve yourself to fit into the latest styles. Plus-size ladies, head to:

- Nordstrom
- Ashley Stewart
- Abby Z.
- Target
- Saks Fifth Avenue
- Victoria's Secret

Tall

These stores offer pants in "long," which is vital for women with mile-long legs. The best places for those women are:

- Express
- Gap
- New York & Company
- JCPenney

Trend Report

The word "trend" might make you nervous. Not one to keep up with the latest fashions, you may be saying to yourself, *I'm not trendy*. Or you might be the girl who wants to wear only the latest trends, mimicking what you see in the spreads of your many favorite fashion magazines. But are those trends, or simply fads? What's the difference? Classic trends are a smart way to get your money's worth from shopping, because these pieces are never out of fashion. Fads, on the other hand, can go out of style in almost as much time as it takes to try them on. And they don't return for a long, long time. I'm not saying you shouldn't have fun with fads. Just don't spend a lot on them. Here's how to tell the difference between trends and fads.

TRENDS VS. FADS

Spend on trends: The fashion reports may say spring is all about the trench. Because of that you'll see wonderful belted raincoats all over the place. But a trench coat is a classic and will serve you way past its "it" season. Same is true with the almighty dress. How many summer or fall seasons have you heard that the dress is back? Guess what? Dresses are amazing no matter what season. So enjoy it when the dress, the trench, the white shirt, or any other classic becomes a trend.

Pass on investing big bucks when it comes to fads: A fad (trucker hats, crystals on teeth, harem pants) is something that might last a season, if that. Unlike a classic trend, fads are usually something novel or a look that hasn't been around in a really long time. Oftentimes they are inspired by genres outside of fashion, such as music, movies, or sports. Beyoncé vintage-style music video for "Naughty Girl" had all of the girls (me included) making a mad dash for cargo pants to sport with stacked heels. Fortunately, I purchased mine for next to nothing at a surplus store.

Attention, Bargain Babes!

Bargain babes don't mind going against the grain when it comes to trends. It can actually benefit your pockets if you shop "off trend." Perhaps you love bright, bold colors, but they're not listed as the Season's Must-Have Trend. Don't give up shopping for (or wearing) them. While everybody is buying black, all the color items will be on sale. Go ahead and make your move. You'll be in style, and for much less, when those beautiful hues come back into vogue.

SHOP TALK WITH . . . **Joyann King,**
fashion editor and writer

> "Don't wear one trend or designer head-to-toe. Mix and match your favorite pieces for a completely original look."

Complete Wardrobe List

The items in your closet should cater to your personal style and body type, but here is a list of everything you need for a great wardrobe foundation. You don't need to run out and buy this all at once. Instead, build up your base over time with quality items.

- **Single-breasted pantsuit or skirt suit:** Whether you work on Wall Street or at the reception desk, wearing a great suit will earn you a great deal of respect. One will do for people who don't work in offices. For business professionals who wear them daily, three or four will "suit" you just fine.
- **Tanks and T-shirts:** In solid white, solid black, solid neutral, and a few colors of choice, they can be a

thin layer to wear under a heavy sweater in the winter or pair with a bright skirt in the summer.

- **Thin camisoles:** In nude and black, layer under sheer items or wear as an underpinning under a suit.

- **Flat-front trousers:** These go-to slacks can be mixed and matched with separates like blazers, blouses, vests, sweaters, and more for work or weekend-evening events.

- **Pencil skirt:** The pencil is forever hot because it sucks you in and smooths the common problem areas around the tummy and butt.

- **Button-down oxford:** Under a shift dress or a cardigan, tied in a knot with a full skirt, over jeans or cigarette pants, the ways to wear this classic are endless.

- **Blouse:** Silk blouses are the perfect way to liven up suits or dress up jeans.

- **Cashmere cardigan:** Worn as your outerwear or even layered under a dress or blazer, cardigans bring life and options to outfits.

- **Single-breasted blazer:** A great way to take the chill off without removing any of your style.

- **Wrap dress:** Don't be shy on these babies . . . they flatter every figure!

- **Little black dress:** The perfect LBD will get you through many fashion pickles. It can actually work for every single style personality and every single event—except a white party.

- **Cool pair of jeans:** Jeans are no longer a lazy or dressed-down alternative. Pair them with heels and diamonds, or pink sneakers and a cashmere hoodie.

- **LCD:** A little colored dress (or little cocktail dress) has the importance of a LBD with a boost! A super easy way to pull off effortless chic.

- **Dressy trouser jeans:** Cut similar to a flat-front wide-leg trouser, they are very forgiving in the bum and thigh area. Dark denim trouser jeans are in demand every season and ideal for casual Fridays in the office and social gatherings.

- **Tailored or belted trench coat:** It's instant chic and a great canvas to play with—changing belts, adding brooches, trying new buttons, or wearing as is.

- **Shapely wool or cashmere coat:** Being warm doesn't have to mean looking like the Michelin Man.

- **Sleek pumps:** In a neutral color of choice like a black, nude, or gray, they are terrific for elongating legs.
- **Ballerina flats:** Simply a stylish and comfortable classic.
- **Stylish sneakers:** Look good while sprinting through your errands.
- **Structured tote:** In a rich vivid color that you like to wear from season to season, like a cognac brown, it's big enough to hold work papers while still looking pulled together.
- **Evening clutch:** The finishing touch to your evening look.
- **Hoop earrings:** They are the LBD of ears. Choose your preferred size and width.
- **Diamond or CZ stud earrings:** A simple, easy way to feel like an heiress.
- **Cocktail ring (real or costume):** The one item that will make your hand look like royalty.
- **Belts:** In ribbon or leather, they pull a look together that was lacking an added element.
- **Scarves:** Like belts, these can bring instant oomph to an outfit.
- **Sleek sweatpants or yoga pants:** Ditch the dated eighties

elastic ankle numbers and treat yourself to a flattering pair.

Now that you've taken a cold hard look at your closet's offerings, the inventory of needed clothes for your Complete Wardrobe List might be a mile long. You've realized you completely need to overhaul your accessories. Your basics need shoring up. And let's not even talk about your lingerie drawer. You are raring to go on a serious shopping mission. But there's just one thing standing in the way of achieving all your fashion goals. That's right—cash. Or the lack of it. If you are like most of us, you don't have a lot of the green stuff to burn on beautiful clothes. That's okay. I'm going to show you how to make the most from the resources you *do* have. I'm not promising you'll be able to check everything off your Complete Wardrobe List in one shopping trip (I don't advise that anyway), but you will find an affordable and fun way to feed your fashion habit.

Budgets and Bargains for Any Babe

GET WHAT YOU WANT WITHOUT GIVING UP A LOT

D o you have Chanel taste with a Dollar Store budget? You might be beyond obsessed with Christian Louboutin and name your first child Roberto Cavalli. However, if your bank account is more Martinelli's than Veuve Clicquot, you're not headed on a million-dollar shopping spree in Paris anytime soon. There's still hope. A lot of hope. It might take a little more work than simply plunking down a gold card, but no matter your budget or your personal style, there is something fantastic to cater to you! Style is no longer limited to how much money you make, or what state you live in . . . It's like we are all residents of the Stylish Home of the Free and Beautifully Brave! God bless the U.S.A.!

First off, there are amazing options at practically every price point. With some expert guidance, you'll find many fashion-forward items for less than a hundred dollars. There are also many high-end fashion designers embracing luxe looks for less with more economical lines in big chain stores. Of course, there's always the almighty sale, where you can snag typically out-of-your-price-range garments on deep discount. But you'll need the tools to know what items and brands are truly bargains. Sometimes it makes the best economic sense to spend a little more on a pair of shoes, a handbag, or a suit if these are keeper pieces you'll return to time and time again. I'll break down the difference between indulgent and investment purchases. I will help you track upcoming sales and manage your seasonal purchases with my ultimate Shopping Planner. Yes, it is possible to keep the bills paid and still look great.

The Hundred-Dollar and Under Club

Long gone are the days when budget shoppers had to wait a season or more for hot items to hit the discount stores.

Amazing retailers with lower price points than traditional boutiques and department stores now crank out the latest styles for a lot less. Stores such as H&M, Topshop, Target, Kohl's, and Payless do their own versions of up-to-the-minute looks. So it's now more than possible to fill your closet with lots of great items for under a hundred dollars from top high-end designers! However, there's no way these chains can deliver the quality of a two-thousand-dollar Versace dress for fifty dollars. Generally, they use cheaper fabrics and pay less attention to detail. But there are some insider style tricks to make that under-a-hundred-dollar piece look like it's worth well over a thousand.

LAYERING

It's amazing what a few light layers can do to a look. Think a piece under and a piece over the core item. You can layer a light tank under a dress under a great little jacket. Don't be afraid to layer jewelry either. Stack necklaces or charm bracelets to create interesting textures and shapes.

DON'T MATCH

Being matchy-matchy—translation: every single thing is red, from your shoes to your undies—says overload and style distress. Instead, go for interesting color combos or those that complement each other, such as navy and pink, or chocolate and Tiffany blue. Try mixing styles as well. If you're doing an ethnic African printed dress, you don't have to wear African beads, an African printed bag, and an African headpiece. Mix it up with a pair of modern hoop earrings and gold gladiator sandals. The unexpected will highlight what's gorgeous about your under-a-hundred-dollar purchase.

ACCESSORIZE RICHLY

It's the oldest trick in the book, but definitely one of the best. Pairing a great investment shoe or bag with simple clothes (even jeans and a T-shirt) will make you look like you just stepped out of your Maybach.

SHOP TALK WITH . . . **Yaniece Thomas,**
designer and stylist for *America's Next Top Model* and Tyra Banks

"When shopping for quality inexpensive items, please keep it simple. Don't go for too many bells and whistles. Also, look for solid colors. They tend to look more expensive!"

Daisy's Obsessions and Steals for $100 or Under

$100	Calvin Klein boots from Endless.com in the middle of the summer
$95	Michael Kors watch from Macy's Memorial Day Sale
$90	Samsonite luggage from Marshalls
$85	Egyptian cotton robe on sale at SoftSurroundings.com
$80	Marc by Marc Jacobs dress from the Barneys Warehouse Sale
$75	designer wallet on markdown at Loehmann's
$70	pair of premium designer jeans in a consignment store
$65	Polo denim jacket from the boy's department of a store
$60	two sets of CK lingerie from T.J. Maxx
$55	cocktail ring from an estate sale
$50	peacoat from the juniors department of a store
$40	nude camisole at La Perla outlet
$35	vintage broach from the flea market
$30	designer umbrella from Filene's Basement
$5	bottle of Rit to dye and update an old white blouse
$5	fashion magazine for free styling advice
$1	yard of ribbon for a quick ribbon belt and headband

Splurge to Save

The price tag should be part of the equation when you are deciding on that killer Gucci dress or a Ferragamo scarf that's as smooth as baby-soft skin. A lot of people shop based exclusively on price—if it's not expensive, they don't want any part of it. On the other side of the fence, some people have an anxiety attack if you even suggest that they take a look beyond the clearance rack. Well-balanced closets have a mix of high- and low-end pieces. And when you are spending your money, whether it is five dollars or five hundred, you need to know why things cost what they do.

HOW FASHION INSIDERS STRETCH A DOLLAR

We aren't the only ones who love a bargain. Saving cash is all the rage these days. Check out how these top stylists, editors, and other experts make their dollars work beautifully for them.

(continued)

Rajni Jacques, *Nylon* magazine fashion editor

- $1 wet n wild eyeliner

Wouri Vice, celebrity fashion stylist for Alicia Keys and Chris Rock

- $1 flip-flops from a local nail salon
- $5 vintage boyfriend-cut jeans from a thrift store

Diana Oberlander, stylist for Madonna, Meg Ryan, Kate Moss, Zoe Saldana, and Chloë Sevigny

- $25 black ballet slippers
- $1 each for hoop earrings, dark mascara, and eyeliner at a 99-cents store

Christian Langbein, handles fashion events and openings for Barneys New York

- $1 vintage T-shirts at a flea market

Yaniece Thomas, stylist for Tyra Banks

- $5 earrings at Claire's
- $1 ribbon to make a cute headband

Julee Wilson, *Real Simple* fashion editor

- $5 Hug My Heels gel liners by Airplus For Her
- 99-cent bobby pins for hair styling

Amy Elisa Keith, *People* magazine writer

- $25 chocolate brown bra from Target's Gilligan & O'Malley line (they match well with different skin tones)
- $1 Palladio blotting paper sheets from CVS to get rid of shiny skin

WHAT'S IN A DESIGNER BRAND?

Many shoppers look at brands as loyal friends that they don't mind paying because they know they can trust them. Others love to flash conspicuous logos that symbolize wealth or status. Some simply want to be in the fashion intelligentsia by wearing a line that's riding a wave of recent press coverage. Not all labels are popular because they have a quality track record in terms of durability, performance, and style. When it comes to designer goods, here's what you are paying for.

Quality

Couture garments cost more (a *lot* more) than ready-to-wear because of the intensive time and labor that go into making each piece—not to mention the skill of the workers. If a piece requires twenty people and three months to make, it will cost far more than an item that's produced by three people in a factory over a couple of hours. Take note of how much labor went into producing the item you are considering. A good place to start is by identifying how many seams are on the garment. The fewer seams an item has, the less work it took to sew. The list can go on and on as far as indicators of an expensive garment, but they include the quality and the feel of the fabric, the smell, how tightly the seams are sewn, the resilience of the material (does it spring back into its original shape once it is tried on and removed from the body?), the notions, and the interior construction of the garment.

Availability and Production

A chic Italian brand sold at only one store in the United States can charge more simply because it's not sold anywhere else. Also, where an item is manufactured contributes to its price because of costs that the brand incurs in producing it (shipping, taxes, labor, etc.), which vary from place to place. Whether an item is produced domestically or internationally will affect the bottom line. Some people revel in this type of exclusivity, while others don't feel it's worth the price.

All Wrapped Up

Everyone loves the pretty labels, fancy-looking hangtags, and special shopping bags that you get at high-end stores. But don't think these are free with purchases. Designers incur charges for everything that has their name on it—including marketing and advertising—and those charges are included in what you pay for the item in the bag.

Location, Location, Location

Brands have to pay for real estate where they're sold. If you shop in a department store where there's a constant rotation of merchandise, an item will often cost less than it would in a specialty boutique, where clothes are kept at full price longer. High-end boutiques also have higher expenses, including higher rent and taxes. It's one reason online shopping can offer discounts on designer labels—websites don't need to maintain expensive storefronts (but they don't always have knowledgeable salespeople either).

Attention, Bargain Babes

It's good to be familiar with a specific brand's price points when shopping sample sales and online sales where an item's original price may not be listed. Once you have an idea of how pieces were originally priced, you'll have a much better chance of scoring smart deals. You can feel better about spending three hundred dollars on a bag if you know that it was originally priced at three thousand. Check out label websites directly to see original pricing.

MONEY/STYLE EQUATION

Are you squirming over the price of a marked-down suit, feeling that it's still just a little too expensive? Consider a style equation:

- Suit costs $600
- You will wear the suit about six times a month, or roughly seventy-two times a year (including when you wear the jacket and skirt separately).
- A great suit will last a good ten years.
- Total wears = 720
- $600 divided by 720 wears = 83 cents per wear!
- Final tally: Run, don't walk to the cash register.

Designer Brands on the Cheap

Getting hip to the fact that most consumers can't afford to spend an entire month's salary on a coat, many designers have come out with lower-priced lines that I like to call Kid Sister Lines. The best part is that they bring the same acute design sense to these lower-priced lines that they bring to their main collections. You can rest assured that these collections are trustworthy, since the designers have reputations to maintain. In order to keep prices low, they'll select less-expensive but still quality fabrics (a silk-rayon blend rather than 100 percent silk, for example) and use labor saving construction and detailing.

It is essential to snag exclusive in-store collections (like the one Jimmy Choo did for H&M, or Anna Sui for Target) as soon as they launch. In fact, if it's your favorite designer, you should be at the store as soon as the doors open, since these special event collections can sell out immediately. I love many of these brands and appreciate the money they save me.

KID SISTER LINES CHEAT SHEET

The naughty girls in high school used cheat sheets on daunting exams and finals. Well, you have my approval to use a Style Cheat Sheet for getting the luxe look for less. In this instance, cheaters actually do win!

What the diamonds mean:

- Two Carat Diamond: ♦ pretty good
- Three Carat Diamond: ♦ amazing!
- Four Carat Diamond: ♦ beyond fabulous!!!

KID SISTER LINES DESIGNED FOR SPECIFIC RETAILERS

Original Line	Rating	Kid Sister Line	Rating
Vera Wang $1000 & over		Simply Vera for Kohls $100 & under	
Isaac Mizrahi $1000 & over		Isaac Mizrahi for Liz Claiborne $100 & under	
Norma Kamali $500 & over		Norma Kamali for Walmart $100 & under	
Lela Rose $300 & over		Lela Rose for Payless $100 & under	
Christian Siriano $500 & over		Christian Siriano for Payless $100 and under	
Abaeté $300 & over		Abaeté for Payless $100 & under	
Jimmy Choo $500 & over		Jimmy Choo for H&M $300 & under	
Alice + Olivia $300 & over		Alice + Olivia for Payless $100 & under	
Converse $100 & under		Converse One Star for Target $100 & under	
7 For All Mankind Jeans $300 & under		Seven7 Jeans for Lane Bryant $100 & under	

Original Line	Rating	Kid Sister Line	Rating
Rachel Roy $300 & over	◆	Rachel Roy for Macy's $100 & under	◆
Chip & Pepper Jeans $300 & under	◇	C7P for JCPenney $100 & under	◇
Liz Lange $300 & under	◆	Liz Lange for Target $100 & under	◆
ABS by Allen Schwartz $300 & over	◇	Allen B. by Allen Schwartz for JCPenney $200 & under	◇
Nicole Miller $300 & over	◆	Nicole by Nicole Miller for JCPenney $100 & under	◇
Matthew Williamson $500 & over	◆	Matthew Williamson for H&M $200 & under	◆
Charlotte Ronson $200 & over	◇	I Heart Ronson for JCPenney $100 & under	◇

DIFFUSION LINES

These are often sold at the same department stores as the pricier original lines, but in different departments.

Original Line	Rating	Diffusion Line	Rating
Donna Karan	♦	DKNY	♦
Calvin Klein Collection	♦	Calvin Klein	♦
BCBGMaxAzria	♦	BCBGeneration	♦
Ralph Lauren	♦	Lauren	♦
Preen	♦	Preen Line	♦
Vivienne Westwood	♦	Vivienne West-wood Anglomania	♦
Oscar de la Renta	♦	O Oscar	♦
Rick Owens	♦	Rick Owens Lilies	♦
Marc Jacobs	♦	Marc by Marc Jacobs	♦
Chloé	♦	See by Chloé	♦
Kenneth Cole	♦	Kenneth Cole Reaction	♦
Prada	♦	Miu Miu	♦
Tracy Reese	♦	Plenty by Tracy Reese	♦

Original Line	Rating	Diffusion Line	Rating
Roberto Cavalli	◆	Just Cavalli	◆
Paul & Joe	◆	Paul & Joe Sister	◆
Vera Wang	◆	Vera Wang Lavender Label	◆
Ralph Lauren	◆	Polo Ralph Lauren	◆
Stella McCartney	◆	adidas by Stella McCartney	◆
Moschino	◆	Moschino Cheap and Chic	◆
Alexander Wang	◆	T by Alexander Wang	◆
HUGO by Hugo Boss	◆	BOSS by Hugo Boss	◆
Michael Kors	◆	MICHAEL Michael Kors	◆
Marchesa Couture	◆	Notte by Marchesa	◆
Missoni	◆	M Missoni	◆
Giorgio Armani	◆	Armani Exchange	◆
Malandrino	◆	Catherine Malandrino	◆
Blumarine	◆	Blugirl Blumarine	◆

COOL COPYCATS

Does a Tory Burch tunic make your heart sing? A Coach tote make you wild? Designers are often as inspired by fantastic styles as we are. That might be why there are so many high-quality inexpensive items that are scarily similar to (and a whole lot less than) their luxe counterparts.

Closeness rating:

😊😊: identical twin

😠😊: fraternal twin

If You Adore	Your Accountant May Prefer	Twin Rating	Average Savings
Christian Louboutin round-toe pumps	Jessica Simpson round-toe pumps	😊😊	$900
Loro Piana cashmere cardigan	J.Crew cashmere cardigan	😠😊	$1200
Narciso Rodriguez pencil skirt	Gap pencil skirt	😊😊	$700
Theory pantsuit	Zara pantsuit	😊😊	$400
Chloé sweater	Sears Apostrophe sweater	😠😊	$900
Tibi party dress	Maggy London party dress	😠😊	$400

If You Adore	Your Accountant May Prefer	Twin Rating	Average Savings
Juicy Couture Flats	Sam Edelman Flats	😛🙂	$250
L.A.M.B. platform heels	Jessica Simpson platform heels	😛🙂	$600
Tory Burch tunic	Blue Plate tunic	😛🙂	$300
Coach tote bag	Banana Republic tote bag	🙂🙂	$300
Rachel Pally jersey tops	Forever 21 jersey top	😛🙂	$100
Ed Hardy tee	Junk Food tee	😛🙂	$80
Burberry quilted jacket	Talbots quilted jacket	😛🙂	$500
Miraclesuit one-piece swimsuit	Newport News Shape fx one-piece swimsuit	😛🙂	$100
Brian Atwood shoes	Nine West shoes	😛🙂	$800
Stuart Weitzman patent colored pumps	Frederick's of Hollywood patent colored pumps	🙂🙂	$250
Tiffany diamond studs	Givenchy cubic zirconia studs	🙂🙂	$2000
Wolford hosiery	DKNY hosiery	🙂🙂	$100
Miss Sixty dark denim skinny jeans	Just USA dark denim skinny jeans	🙂🙂	$250

(continued)

If You Adore	Your Accountant May Prefer	Twin Rating	Average Savings
Roberto Cavalli maxi jersey dress	t-bags maxi jersey dress	😁😊	$1500
Lacoste polo shirt	Aéropostale polo shirt	😁😊	$175
Kate Spade eyewear	A.J. Morgan eyewear	😁😊	$300
Cesare Paciotti shoes	Boutique 9 shoes	😁😊	$900
Polo shirt dress	Lands' End shirt dress	😁😊	$250
Brooks Brothers button-down oxford shirt	Express button-down oxford shirt	😁😊	$100
Giuseppe Zanotti wedges	Bakers wedges; Chinese Laundry wedges	😁😊	$800
Judith Leiber evening clutch	Moyna evening clutch; Santi evening clutch	😁😊	$3000

Tailor Your Budget

The scene: You are in the midst of raging fashion fanatics salivating over every nook and cranny of the amazing Barneys Warehouse Sale. You see them: the Dolce & Gabbana beautiful winter-white cashmere-blend pants from the fall campaign ad. Instantly, everything pauses. The picture is in your screensaver and on your mood board, but they haven't gone on the slightest sale all season. Smiling, you immediately snatch them up and take a deep breath as if you are in a laundry detergent commercial. Your high only gets higher when you see they are marked down from $425 to $125! But wait. You notice the zipper won't move and there's a gap in one of the side seams. The pressure is on because you spot a redhead out of the corner of your eye, style stalking you. You have to make a decision, quick. Do you politely hand the pants over to the redhead, telling her they have her name written all over them, because there's no use in buying anything that's not in mint condition? Or do you snatch them up and march directly to the tailor, where for a total of $25 he replaces the zipper and fixes the seam. I think you know the answer.

Using a tailor can help you cut hemlines *and* costs. The more you explore amazing deals, the more you will come across steals that would be perfect if you could *just* take it in here or there. Here's what you need to know about alterations when checking out less-than-pristine items on sale.

SKIRTS AND PANTS ARE TOO SHORT

Hemlines can be one of the easiest and cheapest alterations. Check the fold at the hem and see how much extra
fabric is folded under, usually about a half to one inch.
Make sure there is enough fabric above the seam to give
you the length you need. Depending on the fabric and
style, some tailors will be able to add additional fabric
onto the bottom by adding a seam.

SKIRTS AND PANTS ARE TOO LONG

Skirts and pants, even shorts and dresses, are usually
easy to shorten. Consider the shape of the bottom of the
item. For example, if it's a pencil skirt, you're fine. But
if the skirt has a special bottom, like a fluted or tulip
bottom, it can be a challenge to shorten. Challenges are
green lights for tailors to charge you more for their service.

SHOULDERS OF A BLAZER ARE TOO BIG

It's doable to take them in if you check the lining and
find the shoulders are enlarged by shoulder pads or by
excess fabric.

IT'S TOO SNUG IN THE WAIST

For a little extra wiggle room, sometimes all you need is a quarter of an inch.

IT'S TOO BIG IN THE WAIST

Darts are popular solutions to take in items at the waist, especially for women who wear different sizes in skirts vs. pants because of their hips.

IT'S TOO SNUG IN THE THIGHS

Like the waist, if there is enough room on the seam allowance (the extra fabric on the inside of the seam), it can be let out for a little extra breathing room.

A ZIPPER DOESN'T WORK

Zippers can be replaced. The only issue may be if you are trying to repair or replace a special-color zipper or a zipper handle with a designer logo or emblem on it. Before resorting to replacing the zipper, check for loose threads or tags that could be stuck inside and causing hesitation. They can be removed or picked out with tweezers.

A BUTTON IS MISSING

No problemo! Once you see how easy this is to repair, you might even want to do this yourself. Check out the DIY resources at the back of the book for places to get cool buttons in the notions department.

THERE IS A HOLE IN THE GARMENT

If the hole is on the seam, and there is a gap in the middle of the seam, this is really easy to fix. If there is an actual hole in the fabric, it can be repaired depending on the material. Knits can be mended together, and leather and suede can be patched. But these repairs can be costly and complicated. You can always consider adding a design cover-up, like a brooch or additional button.

Accessories 101

Accessories are such a pivotal part of looking amazing that I call them the costars of your outfit—the ones that always end up stealing the spotlight! They can dress up the simplest black dress and really extend the outfits in your wardrobe. If you're going to spend money on anything in your wardrobe, shoes and bags should be, respectively, number one and two on your list. Just be sure to leave enough extra change for water, because you'll need to stay fully hydrated in order to thank everyone for all the compliments you're going to receive.

Whenever possible, buy the real deal when it comes to shoes and bags. I do not believe in endorsing obvious knockoffs. There is nothing worse than seeing a girl with a bag that's supposed to be Chanel, except "Chanel" is spelled with two Ns! And don't get me started on the really bad knockoffs, like the ones that have double Gs instead of double Cs. Women now have unprecedented access to online sample sales, end-of-season sales, and designer out-lets, which means that even if your salary is far from six figures, you can acquire amazing designer shoes and bags. I must also give a nod to lower-end designers who have stepped up their design departments. It's perfectly fine to purchase a shoe or a bag inspired by a high-end designer.

Since shopping options are literally everywhere, it is important to be smart about your accessory choices. Don't pay $150 for a mid-level shoe brand when you can wait for the original designer style to go on sale and pay $165. If you see a great sandal in a lower-priced store that looks identical to the high-end label, and it's less than the tax on the high-end shoe, scoop it up. And while you're at it, see if they have other colors in your size!

When evaluating bags, shoes, jewelry, and other accessories, consult the same mental checklist that you use when shopping for clothing. Always be aware of special exaggerations on an accessory like a major high wedge or an enormously large bow. Extraordinary details like that can boost the price of an item. Here are a few elements you should specifically pay attention to when shopping for accessories:

HANDBAGS

Pay close attention to the bag's hardware, including rivets, D-rings, and studs. Does it feel heavy? Heft is generally a sign of high quality . . . Sorry, girls, your shoulder's going to get a workout. Consider it cute cardio! Unless it's intentionally distressed, metal hardware should have a nice shine or matte finish, and be scratch, blemish, and blotch free.

BELTS

Buckles made from rare materials like ivory or real tortoiseshell and belts made from exotic skins will add to the value of the piece.

SHOES

The shape and structure of a heel and toe are surefire ways to tell a quality keeper from a not-so-great cheapie. Avoid cheap cork, wood, and plastic. Lucite is strong and very different from plastic. And toe cleavage is a common trait in better quality shoes.

JEWELRY

Nonmetal elements such as wood, beads, patent, resin, Lucite, and PVC are available in low- and high-end pieces and are sometimes very similar in appearance. I just adore places like Forever 21, H&M, and Target for low-end stylish jewelry. For a real education in jewelry, study the work of my favorite designers, Kenneth Jay Lane, Erickson Beamon, and Patricia von Musulin.

SCARVES

Do a softness inspection by rubbing the material on your cheek. Reject anything that feels even the slightest bit rough. One hundred percent silk and cashmere are great investments. They are as durable as they are lovely.

Seasonal Shopping Sheet

Now that you have a clear vision of what you will be searching for, you are ready to fill out your Seasonal Shopping Sheet. This source will keep you on a successful shopping track and help you conquer as many bargains as possible. Use the sample below to create your own Seasonal Shopping Sheet. Have your mood board handy for inspiration as you fill out one sheet for spring and one for fall. Try your hardest to stick to your shopping sheet, so that your budget remains under control. Never be caught without your shopping sheet (keep a copy in your desk and bag or on your phone)—you never know when you will stumble upon a great sale.

SAMPLE SEASONAL SHOPPING SHEET:

Overall Inspiration

Season:

Style Icon:

Celeb Inspiration:

Style Goal:

Monthly Shopping Budgets

Monthly Budget $_____

Pay Days:____/____/____ & ____/____/____

Monthly Sales:_____

Dates:____/____/____ , ____/____/____

Locations:_____

Confirmed in Calendar:_____

Monthly Budget $_____

Pay Days:____/____/____ & ____/____/____

Monthly Sales:_____

Dates:____/____/____ , ____/____/____

Locations:_____

Confirmed in Calendar:_____

Monthly Budget $_____

Pay Days:____/____/____ & ____/____/____

Monthly Sales:_____

Dates:____/____/____ , ____/____/____

Locations:_____

Confirmed in Calendar:_____

Total Shopping Budget for the Season: $_____

Replenishers List:

1._____ Approximate Cost:$_____

2._____ Approximate Cost:$_____

Wardrobe Holes:

1._____

2._____

Seasonal Must-Haves:

1._____

2._____

3._____

New Designers to Try:

1._____

2._____

Attach any photos, coupons, sale announcements, salespersons' business cards.

A little planning goes a long way when it comes to shopping. Armed with your Seasonal Shopping Sheets, you've got the information at your fingertips to keep you from getting talked into yet another pair of black classic pumps. There's no reason to be instantly afraid of high-end designer labels. You know they can be a bargain if the item is a classic (and on markdown) because you'll wear it over and over. At the same time, if your budget is only a dollar, there are tons of things you can do with that single bill to look a lot cuter. You are the real educated consumer. But what happens when you actually enter a store? Will you lose your mind at the first sign of a big red sale sign? You'd better not! The breadth and depth of shopping today can be dizzying. I'm going to take you through every kind of retail experience so that when you finally walk through those mall doors or click on that website, you'll be prepared in true Bargain Babe style.

Hitting the Shops 4

Growing up in Los Angeles, I loved reading *Sweet Valley High* books, going to the beach, and shopping, shopping, shopping! Hunting for cute clothes was my weekend hobby, and my after-school hobby too. As a fashion-hungry teen, I was so addicted to the Nordstrom juniors department, Brass Plum, that I became a member of their secret fashion society, the BP Club! But I didn't stop there. I scoured the racks of outlets, vintage stores, and everything in between. As a self-proclaimed shopaholic since birth, I have learned that department stores, discount stores, even airport stores have many overlooked and underappreciated perks. We'll start with my old stomping ground, the department store, and then hit every possible place you can shop smart, spend less, and look your best.

Department Stores

When you hit your favorite department store, you should always check out its private label. Every major department store has specific private labels that cater to each department's key customer. Not only do they cater to the shopper's demographic, but they are much cheaper than their in-store competition. The private label will always reflect the design aesthetics of the designer labels the store carries—but without taking on the high-end price. With their private labels, department stores handle their own production, design, and distribution, which eliminates a lot of the costs big-name designers have to include in their prices. But they don't scrimp when it comes to style. By taking runway trends and translating them specifically for the taste of their customer, private labels can cover both the classics and easier-to-wear interpretations of current trends. Even better, the private labels are not exempt from markdowns, so you usually end up paying even less than you would for the marked-down designer pieces.

DEPARTMENT STORE PRIVATE LABELS

Look out for these private labels in your favorite department stores.

Macy's

- INC
- Charter Club
- Style & Co.
- Alfani
- Martha Stewart Collection
- Greendog (kids)
- Epic Threads (kids)

Bloomingdale's

- Aqua

Nordstrom

- Nordstrom
- Caslon
- Semantiks
- Rubbish

Lord & Taylor

- Black Brown (men)
- Kate Hill (women)

Dillard's

- Gianni Bini
- Antonio Melani

Barneys New York

- Barneys New York
- Barneys CO-OP

Neiman Marcus

- Neiman Marcus

Every department store has a juniors department, and it's typically filled with senior-level style potential! Don't worry. You won't end up looking like your kids. The juniors department and the boys section offer fashion-forward and classic items such as cool T-shirts and cashmere sweaters. The prices are really reasonable (since department store buyers try to keep them lower for young people), and the sales are always a mega hit. Finding a well-fitting piece in the boys department works best if you have a small upper body (ranging from a size zero to six). Go for the larger sizes in boys for a modern, shrunken look. The juniors department will be filled with a lot of brands that you may not be familiar with, but they are big on style. It can be great for trying shapes and trends that you aren't sure you want to invest a lot of money in. It's also a great resource for finding items to mix with your high-end pieces and accessories.

FOR THE KID IN YOU

Here are some great pieces to look for in the juniors and boys departments.

- *Costume jewelry:* hoops, novelty bracelets, and charms
- *Shrunken collegiate blazers:* navy versions with beautiful classic gold buttons are well stocked year-round.
- *Cashmere pullovers:* Ralph Lauren has the best cashmere for kids: same quality, at a fraction of the adult-size versions' prices that will rock your world.
- *Cashmere socks:* I love the versions in colorful argyle.
- *Graphic tees*
- *Cropped jackets*

SHOP TALK WITH . . . **a division manager for Macy's**

"Department stores have higher turnover for promotions and sales. We are able to offer sales on items that specialty boutiques might still have at full price because of our size. At Macy's we offer a tourist discount, which covers the sales tax difference for out-of-state shoppers. And if you purchase a gift for someone out of state, in person, some gift registry departments will waive the shipping cost . . . Every second week of the month, we mark down our private labels, and the following third week of the month, the new merchandise from the private labels arrives."

Attention, Bargain Babes

A lot of the major department stores have discounted outlet stores and even blowout warehouse sales with the same quality merchandise that they previously carried in-store! See the shopping guide for the discounted outlet of your favorite department store.

Specialty Fashion Boutiques

A lot of women are intimidated by shopping in specialty boutiques because of the occasional intense salesgirls and fears of crazy prices, but they really shouldn't be. Specialty fashion boutiques carry a much smaller stock than major department stores, but they also usually offer a lot of hip, new designers and styles. That means you can always find unique pieces that you won't see anywhere else. You can have a truly luxe shopping experience in these little stores. For example, boutiques, like department stores, hold trunk shows and special fashion shows. But going to one of these shows in a smaller space feels like an exclusive experience where you can actually get a front-row seat to see the collection and sometimes meet the designer.

Because of the smaller environment, it is easier to get personal with the owner and sales associates. The owner is usually the buyer or closely linked to the buyer, and can cater to your style preferences. When you are a repeat loyal customer, the buyer will order items with you in mind and alert you regularly when pieces arrive and go on sale. When you get really close with the owners, you might suggest hosting a special shopping party with your friends to preview the new fall collection or the launch of a new designer for the store. It's a fair trade: You're offering new clientele in exchange for being the first one to get your hands on new pieces! You can score fantastic deals at larger specialty boutiques, like Intermix, Lisa Kline, and LF, which hold end-of-season warehouse sales for the merchandise that they carry. Be sure to get on your favorite boutique's mailing list so that you'll be invited to special events and will be among the first to hear about new products and upcoming sales.

SHOP TALK WITH . . . **Evelyn Ungvari, owner of Diavolina boutique in Los Angeles, where stars such as Cameron Diaz, Halle Berry, and Mandy Moore shop**

"A girl on a budget can have success by making friends with sales associates and being the first to be called when sales start. It's tough competing with department stores, but I wouldn't want my clients buying from me at full price and then seeing it on sale the next day somewhere else."

Chain Stores

Mainstream chain stores like Gap, Ann Taylor, and Express are great when it comes to things like convenience and consistent savings. These stores are totally reliable. You know that every summer J. Crew will have a sundress in a great bright hue and that Ann Taylor will always have a timeless shift dress. And you can't beat the never-ending roster of locations. If you are shopping and you need a different size or color, the sales staff can always check the computerized inventory and tell you exactly which locations have what you need and how many are in stock. They may even offer to call the store and have it held for you. And when it comes to sales, it seems like chain stores are having one every day. Promotions are ongoing, influencing shoppers to buy more and save tons.

DAISY'S FAVORITE CHAIN STORE ITEMS

No matter the season, month, or latest fashion craze, here are some best bets from a chain store near you.

Banana Republic: quality suiting and separates

Express: flat-front timeless classic trousers

Club Monaco: great tanks and T-shirts

Forever 21, Zara, and H&M: up-to-the-minute trend pieces

Old Navy: adorable kids' clothing

J.Crew: candy-colored cardigans and perfect pencil skirts

Target: limited-edition lines from top designers

Attention, Bargain Babes

When you purchase an item from a chain store, hold on to your receipt and pop into the store fourteen days later to check if the item you purchased has gone on sale or been marked down any lower than what you paid for it. If it has, the cashier will give you the difference in cash, and you can shop more! Standard price adjustment time is usually fourteen days, but always double-check a store's policy.

Discount Stores

Imagine walking into a massive fashion tornado and finding gems and treasures tossed everywhere from the storm. That's the experience of discount store shopping, where merchandise that doesn't sell in department stores, back stock from too-large orders, discontinued items, and more wind up at 30 to 90 percent off full price.

I've weathered many storms and have lots of deals to prove it. It's hard for me to choose my best one. Maybe it was when I fed my swimsuit addiction at Loehmann's, where I snapped up a pair of Chloé and Calvin Klein bikinis for under $130 combined! I got my very first pair of Manolo Blahniks at Century 21, and nine years later I still love those cranberry patent leather boots. At Daffy's I found a gorgeous cream-colored Helmut Lang coat. My boss bought the exact same coat at a department store for a *lot* more money. And there has never been a day that I stepped into T.J. Maxx without eyeing their home section for designer home goods. It's so easy to spoil your family at bath time when you've saved tons of money on Ralph Lauren towels.

Although most discount stores don't have the pristine merchandising or posh amenities of more expensive retailers, you'll find all the top designers, including Fendi, Manolo Blahnik, Miu Miu, BCBG, and tons more. The big issue is braving the massive amounts of merchandise you'll encounter. Despite many price-tag temptations, it's essential to shop with the same style standards and integrity as you would at a high-end boutique. Follow these tips to shop discount stores without getting lost in the storm.

- **Have a strategy.** Since there's a lot of ground to cover, go directly to the sections that never fail you, such as accessories, undies, and kids' clothing. It's always best to start on a positive note. Then identify the designer sections, sometimes tucked away on a hidden floor, and head straight for the good stuff.

- **Be patient** as you go through the seemingly neverending racks. Discount stores are no place to go when you are short on time or energy. You need to methodically plow through sections to find your designer steal—preferably aisle by aisle. Random browsing will only confuse you, and you'll wind up looking at the same clothes over and over.

- **Don't be swayed** by red clearance stickers. Editing has to be your partner in crime when shopping discount stores. To edit means to keep some pieces and pass on others. Don't waste time on subpar items just because they are crazy cheap—stick to good labels and fabrics. Try to picture yourself wearing the items you pick out. If you can't get a mental image (or you don't like what you see), put them back.

- **If you like it, buy it.** The great thing about discount stores is that they always have different merchandise. But you never know if they're going to get one DVF dress or twenty. If you see a good deal—that also looks great on you—take advantage! These stores have a high turnover rate, so you have to seize opportunities when they come up. Plus, you can always return that dress or shirt if you have second thoughts in front of the mirror at home.

- **More and more discount stores are stepping things up by offering special perks** typically available only at department stores, like free personal shopping and assistance in finding your size. Don't be afraid to ask the salespeople for help.

- **Some mega discount stores get daily shipments**, which mean daily savings for you. Ask the manager what time the truck arrives and what time they bring out merchandise, to be the first to get your hands on the most popular items.

Outlets

Practically all designers have outlets, stores where manufacturers sell their products directly to the public. There are tons of merchandise and bargains to be had, but it's essential to have a plan before you hit these out-of-the-way shopping meccas.

- **Always check which stores are in the outlet mall before going.** Make sure there are enough brands you like before making the trip, since most outlets are in remote areas.
- **Research the brands online ahead of time** to familiarize yourself with the full retail prices. This way you will know when you have found a bargain at the outlet.
- **Create a shopping plan for the day and map out your route.** I suggest going to the most popular high-end stores first. If you have to choose between Chanel and the Gap, Chanel it is. If that's too much advance planning for you, grab a map at guest services as soon as you arrive.

- **Check that the stores you are going to are actual outlets, and not a store in an outlet mall.** You can get tricked and assume that all the stores are outlets, but sometimes they are not.

- **Shop outlets on weekdays** and stay away from Monday holidays and weekends, when the crowds are massive.

- **Outlet stores also have clearance racks** with additional markdowns. Like in most retail stores, they are usually located toward the back. Merchandise closer to the front is made up of the newer arrivals.

- **Have a hearty energy-filled breakfast and pack portable energy snacks.** I'm not kidding! The amount of time, money, and energy that you can spend in the food court should be spent on shopping.

Attention, Bargain Babes

If you are in an outlet and aren't sure whether an item is a real bargain, do a spot price comparison while in the store by going to TheFind.com (you'll need a phone with the Internet). The website will pull up the price for any item in the online shopping world.

BONUS SAVINGS FOR ANY STORE

Don't limit coupons and specials to the grocery store. Tons of fashion retailers and websites offer extra discounts if you're resourceful.

Hotels

Ask the concierge or front desk agents if they have any shopping coupons or amenities (e.g., get a free gift with a purchase). If your hotel has an information stand, check it for pamphlets and travel guide booklets with coupons and deals. Some cities have shopping tours that offer special promotions to participants.

Visitor's Bureau

Check your local visitor's bureau's website for traveler discounts to the city you are visiting. Macy's offers all out-of-towners a special discount (you'll need ID).

Friends-and-Family Days

Many chain stores, such as Foot Locker and Armani Exchange, have friends-and-family sales. Check with the store's staff for details on the next round of sales. Some employees also get a standing discount. If you are really committed, get a part-time or seasonal job around Christmas or Thanksgiving for extra cash and savings.

(continued)

Coupons

Department stores and other retailers have mailing lists to send out special discount notices, exclusive shopping times for sales, and more savings opportunities.

Check the Paper

Always check the lifestyle sections of your local paper for printed coupons and discounted shopping news.

Savings Cards

Stores like Loehmann's have special discount cards for customers, offering birthday discounts, points earned for purchases, and news on shipments.

Websites

One of my favorite websites for bargain hunting is StyleBakery.com, which offers additional savings and promotions for many popular stores and brands under its Sweet-Savings tab. Sweet indeed.

Associations and Clubs

AAA offers special discounts to their members on sites like Target.com, Payless, and New York & Company, Students, teachers, government workers, and members of the military are often granted special reductions. So if you are a member of any of these groups, always check if a store has any discounts that apply to you before completing the purchase.

Sample Sales

The ritual of the private press sample sales was brutal when I worked at Condé Nast. For one high-end shoe sale in particular—where only selected editors received a Golden Invite—it was fashion combat at its fiercest. The super-eager girls would faithfully arrive at the sale at least three hours in advance to line up for the numbered ticket that granted them access. The girls who arrived late turned green with envy when they were greeted with the sight of hundreds of assistants (their bosses' shoe orders tucked into their bags) already lined up. Tension continued to build as the opening time approached. When the doors were unlocked, the race began. The most aggressive fashion bandits ravished through the clothes like starved beasts, snapping at anyone who tried to peek into their pickings. Soon the editing process began, and major noise from haggling for sizes and colors filled the room.

Most sample sales are not quite as extreme. But they can still be anxiety-provoking. More than at any other kind of sale, you need to do your homework. The big price you pay for getting such a great deal at sample sales is that you're stuck with your purchase. There are no returns or exchanges ever. Sometimes it's hard to try on the items, which makes shopping even trickier. Know your size in the brand that's having the sale by trying on a selection of clothes in a store beforehand. Take a few notes down just in case you need them as reference. Although the sample sale will most likely not have exactly the same items you've tried on before, a brand stays true to their cut. When you are preparing for a sample sale by researching at a department store, also take note of the retail prices. Don't waste your sample sale time on items that are not at least 30 percent cheaper than retail. If an item is priced similarly to what you'd find in a brick and mortar store, make your purchase there, where you can always return if you have a change of heart.

While we are on the topic of money, the worst sample sale moments happen when you catch a sudden case of amnesia and forget your budget. You can walk in with $200 in cash and leave with a $60 IOU to your coworker and a $250 charge on your "emergency" AmEx. Be aware of your completed Seasonal Shopping Sheet—where I hope you have budgeted for your sample sale shopping—and stick to your limit. There will be sample sales in the future, so no need to blow your life savings on just one.

When it comes to expensive and popular designers, plan to arrive early at the sale, since the serious Bargain Babes will be camped out Madonna-concert-ticket style. I had friends who stayed in the same hotel as one sample sale the night before so they could roll out of bed and be first at the door. And for good reason. I was an early bird at one of Jimmy Choo's first sample sales, where I found a beautiful bag, which originally retailed for $1,300, priced at $200 because of a loose handle that I later repaired for under twenty bucks. Score!

At sample sales, getting first dibs is good. Greed is also very good. Grab as much as you possibly can, piling everything in your arms, teeth, feet, whatever you need to do to hold it all. Remember, this is far, far away from leisurely shopping. Sizes, colors, and styles are limited, and so is your time! Don't be afraid to be a style stalker. If you see a girl pick up your dress—yes, *your* dress—two seconds before you could get your hands on it, don't give up. Keep shopping, but don't let her out of your sight. It's best to stay no farther away than the distance of about two Marc Jacobs bags at all times, so if she drops the dress, you can swoop it up.

Attention, Bargain Babes

One year I was completely stressed out because I'd been working like crazy on one of our biggest issues at *InStyle,* and I hadn't had time to go to the famous Prada/Miu Miu sample sale. Finally I got to leave the office before the sun went down and ran over to the sale, where I discovered that being last is not always that bad. Everything had been marked down from the original sample sale prices. My friend and I got the exact same sandals, but mine were cheaper because she went on the first day. Always pay attention to how many days a sample sale will last. You may not get that season's hot-ticket item, but you'll find a super bargain. Many sales will drop their prices as the days go by, with the lowest of lowest markdowns on the last day.

UNDRESS CODE

I have been to sample sales so good that the girls were shopping practically naked. A lot of times there aren't any dressing rooms at sample sales. If you aren't much of an exhibitionist, you need to wear clothes that are easy to slip in and out of so you can quickly change between the racks.

Clothes

Choose something like a jersey T-shirt dress, so you can try pants or skirts on easily or push it down around your waist while trying blouses.

Shoes

Wear backless thong sandals or any shoes that slip off. No laces please, and don't even think about boots!

Underwear

Opt for nude smooth boycuts and a bralette, or a tank that you feel comfortable exposing to others.

Online Shopping

These are the stores that never close. With the Internet, you can shop 24 hours a day, 365 days a year. And the scope of your shopping is limitless. You can search right around your corner or overseas for any item in any size, color, or price. The must-have bag of the season may not be available in your town, but with your secret weapon—

the search engine—you can have it shipped to your front door within days.

The convenience of online shopping is no secret to anyone with a computer. But fashion on the web has become much more sophisticated than simply JCrew.com. There are services offered for free that will show you what to wear for a cocktail party or a belly dancing class. Some websites will pack a virtual suitcase for your trips—you just have to let them know where you are going and for how many days. Bloggers give fresh outlooks, insider discounts, the latest celebrity style spotting, and more.

Nothing beats the web for comparison shopping. The Internet is simply the smartest way to find your desired pieces at the best price. You can be a Fashion Superhero, searching twenty different sites for fifty designers in minutes! Super bionic powers are the norm when shopping online.

GREAT DEALS, JUST A CLICK AWAY

- Shop at the stroke of midnight, when new sales begin and new merchandise is posted.
- There are online sales on the same days as major department store sales like Black Friday. While all the world and their ances-

tors are waiting at the mall doors in the freezing cold chanting "Open! Open!" you can take advantage of the same savings from under your cozy covers.

- Bookmark your favorite sites and create folders to house them. Name these folders according to the search, such as "Bridesmaid Shoe Options" or "Wardrobe Replenishers." This will save you so much time when going back to sites that you like.

- The web is great for shoppers who are plus-size, have a wide foot, or are looking for any kind of hard-to-find size. Many websites offer extended sizes that are not usually fully stocked or available in stores.

- If you're not sure what size you are in something, order a few sizes. You can always return what you don't need, as most sites have a generous return and shipping policy. Online shoe stores like Endless.com have both free shipping and free returns, so it's just like you are being helped by a shoe salesman when you have several options to try on at home.

- Keep a tape measure handy so you can plug in or compare your measurements with websites that list size charts and measurements. Some even show you a mock version of your body with your actual body measurements on the screen.

SHOP TALK WITH . . . **Lisa Letarte**
Cabrinha, swimwear designer

"The easiest style of swimsuit to buy online is a slide triangle top and tie-side bottom—it can be easily adjusted. A suit that has to fit precisely, like one that is structured or has molded cups, is better tried on in stores. It's also good to try a one-piece on in the store, because body lengths can always differ. In terms of fit, make sure you take into consideration the sizing of the brand. Don't be afraid to e-mail the company and ask if the brands you are trying on typically run bigger or smaller. Everyone has their own sizing system—one company's size six can be another company's size eight."

DAISY'S FAVORITE SHOPPING SITES

Best Sites for Comparison Shopping

- ShopStyle.com (they'll notify you when your watched item's price drops)
- TheFind.com
- Shopzilla.com

Best Sites for Deals on Designer Accessories

- Bluefly.com
- eBay.com
- Endless.com
- theOutnet.com

Celeb Looks for Less

- ShopTheLook.net
- PeopleStyleWatch.com
- Instyle.com

Best Site for Finding International Brands

- ASOS.com
- Topshop.com

Best Sites for Advice on What to Wear

- StyleBakery.com
- ClosetCouture.com (they have live stylists to help and pack and style from your actual closet!)

Best Sites for Sales News

- LuckyBreaksOnline.com
- Elle.com
- RunwayRealway.com

(continued)

Best Members-Only Shopping Sites for Designer Pieces

- Gilt.com
- ideeli.com
- HauteLook.com

Best Blog

- Fashionweekdaily.com
- WhoWhatWear.com

Best Sites for Shipping Amenities

- Endless.com (next-day shoes!)
- Amazon.com
- Zappos.com

Best Sites for Bonus Savings and Coupons

- TheBudgetFashionista.com

SHOP TALK WITH . . . Jennifer Davidson and Beth Herbst, the founders of StyleBakery.com

"Scan sites like RetailMeNot.com and Sweet-Savings.com for exclusive discounts before you shop. Also, be sure to check out the sale section of a retailer's site—you can find incredible bargains on in-season items, usually with a much better selection than the sale racks at brick and mortar stores. Another way to find amazing deals is to shop online outlets such as Bluefly.com, YOOX.com, and theOutnet.com (from luxury retailer Net-A-Porter.com) that offer a selection of luxury brands at deep discounts. You can often find the same items that are in department stores, in boutiques, and within the pages of your favorite magazines at much lower prices. For non-fashion items, check out Overstock.com and SmartBargains .com. There's a new way to shop that's growing in popularity: special members-only online sample sale communities like TheTopSecret.com, Gilt.com, and Ideeli.com. They e-mail members whenever there's a new, deeply discounted, online designer sale."

Catalogs

One of the oldest ways to shop is through catalogs. I love to get them in the mail, circling or highlighting the hundreds of items I fantasize about buying at once. You can't try the clothes on before purchasing, just like with online shopping, so you need to consider the cut of pieces, as well as understand the item description. Gorgeous models can make the most horrific outfit look beautiful. Sometimes it will simply be a case of trial and error. Other times, you can check out the clothes in stores first. Most catalogs have kept up with the times by going online as well. But when it comes to my favorite catalogs, such as Victoria's Secret, Spiegel, Newport News, Boden, La Redoute, and Soft Surroundings, nothing beats the experience of thumbing through good old-fashioned paper.

When shopping international catalogs it's important to make the translation so you don't get burned with expensive returns. Consider the origin of the catalog and how their sizing is presented. Before you confirm any purchase, be sure to make the conversion to U.S. dollars. That dress might be a lot more expensive once you do.

Attention, Bargain Babes

Teen catalogs have made getting cute stuff for less a lot more accessible. Among millions of catalogs, teen versions like dELiA's and Alloy are my top picks for finding great trendy bargains. They're similar to shopping in the juniors department. You can find fun pieces in bold colors and great shapes for much less than in catalogs that cater to adults. Don't be thrown off by the teen models. Take into consideration that juniors clothes are cut slimmer than women's, so if you order a six and it doesn't fit, don't immediately assume you've put on a few pounds and go on a hunger strike. You just need to go up a size or two.

Vintage, Thrift, and Consignment Stores

Once when I was at *Essence*, I must have been having a Mother Teresa moment, because I revealed my top-secret favorite vintage store to a girl in the model bookings department. She returned to work the following day complaining that she didn't find anything and that the shop was terrible. Her loss. Shopping for clothes that have already been worn is not for everyone. It takes patience, creativity, and vision.

Shopping this genre is different from shopping in traditional stores, so you should give yourself some time to ease into the experience. Don't feel discouraged if you don't like the first stores that you enter. Keep trying. Vintage, thrift, and consignment stores all have different merchandising and different atmospheres. As with a tailored coat from the sixties, once you find the place that fits your style, you'll know.

WHICH STORE IS RIGHT FOR YOU?

It's important to know what kind of shopping setting you can handle. Some women will shop only in really neat stores with well-edited merchandise that they know caters to their personal style. On the other hand, some people don't mind going to vintage or thrift warehouses where you dig through piles and piles of clothes than can cost as little as a quarter!

Once you know your tolerance for sorting and sifting, you can figure out which stores work for you (see the appendix for a list of vintage, thrift, and consignment stores). Don't throw a fit if you walk into a vintage store and see a Dior blouse for four hundred dollars. There are some vintage and consignment stores that sell really expensive pieces for less, but the price can still be high. The prices should be significantly less than the full retail value, but keep in mind that some people collect vintage fashion the way others collect art. That can lead to some hefty price tags, especially for iconic or important pieces.

VINTAGE STORES

These shops sell pieces from different eras that may or may not have been worn. There are stores that cater to designer pieces only, with major labels like Dior and Yves

Saint Laurent from previous seasons. Red carpet A-listers such as Penélope Cruz and Reese Witherspoon love sporting vintage to major award shows because they don't have to worry about seeing someone else in the same dress.

The Ideal Vintage Customer:

- You like looking different.
- You appreciate the craftsmanship of vintage pieces.
- You appreciate fashion history.
- You are always looking for a bargain.

THRIFT STORES

Also referred to as secondhand stores, they sell used pieces that have been donated. The proceeds from these sales usually go to charity. There are mass chain thrift stores (like Salvation Army) in huge warehouses and smaller, private thrift sellers in church basements or tucked away on street corners.

The Ideal Thrift Store Customer:

- You're up for the challenge of creating a great look for next to nothing.
- You're not squeamish.

- You don't necessarily follow the latest trends but prefer to create your own.
- You like wearing pieces from the era where current trends came from.
- You like giving back, especially when you, well, get a little in return.

CONSIGNMENT STORES

Also referred to as resale stores, they sell pieces on behalf of individuals who bring their clothing in to make money. Pieces are usually current, or from the last year or two, although occasionally a vintage piece will be available. What consignment shops buy from sellers really depends on what's popular locally.

The Ideal Consignment Shop Customer:

- You want access to current pieces at less than retail prices, and don't mind if they've been worn a few times.

SHOP TALK WITH . . . **Micaela Beckwith,**
senior editor and buyer for Hollywood A-listers' fave _Decades Two_

"Consigning is really a science and Decades has truly mastered it. We match the consigner with the shopper. I shop for my shoppers, which is everyone from the sixteen-year-old schoolgirl to the thirty-year-old housewife. As a shopper, get to know your match and their consignor number. If consigner #679 is a size 6 shoe, we can call you when she drops off a load of shoes if you are a size 6, too! Another large part of the business now is dealing with a store's end-of-season stock and full-size run of shoes. A shoe that didn't do so well in Houston could be the most coveted shoe in Los Angeles. Sixty percent of our merchandise is brand new with tags, in impeccable condition."

Attention, Bargain Babes

The trendier the area, the higher the vintage store prices. If you are looking for low, low, I mean under-a-dollar-low vintage and thrift store prices, you might want to shop in areas where the locals aren't considered very fashion forward. Small college towns or rural areas can have a wealth of hidden thrifting treasures.

INSPECTOR GADGET

No matter whether shopping vintage or consignment, you'll want to check for a few things before purchasing anything used. There is nothing worse than waving proudly to your date in your new vintage frock, only to feel a cool breeze on your armpit. Even gently used items need a thorough inspection.

Smell

The underarms are first in line for the sniff test. Then take an overall deep inhale of the entire piece. Always wash and dry-clean pieces before wearing them, or you and your closet may get that not-so-nice "vintage smell." Woolite is great for delicates.

Tug

Give a few gentle tugs on the seams or any attached elements such as beads, straps, or zippers. Pieces will often have loose seams that need to be repaired before wearing, so don't pull too hard or you may rip clothes to shreds.

Turn

Always turn the piece inside out to inspect the interior view of the garment. Check for stains or tears in the lining and any surprises like cigarette burns.

FOUR TIPS FOR FIRST-TIME VINTAGE SHOPPERS

Designer Trina Turk—whose clothes are worn by stars such as Jennifer Aniston, Cameron Diaz, and Tori Spelling—loves to comb through vintage collections and wants to help vintage virgins get started.

1. Accessories are a good way to start: Belts, jewelry, and handbags are all great. You can find easy evening bags that are very chic and unique.
2. When you're buying something not precisely your size, go for something bigger rather than too small. Letting out a garment is harder. Taking it in is better.
3. Buy vintage pieces that relate to the trends now.
4. Mix modern and vintage pieces when creating an outfit or look.

Garage Sales, Sidewalk Sales, Flea Markets, and Estate Sales

One man's trash is another woman's treasure. Never underestimate shopping on asphalt, a patch of grass, or even a smooth concrete sidewalk. When I tell you Bargain Babes can shop anywhere, I mean that. Smart strategy for shopping garage sales and their counterparts is very similar to vintage and thrift store shopping. Going in with an open mind is the secret to shopping success. Trips to the Fairfax Flea Market in Los Angeles and the Chelsea Flea Market in New York City are a weekend ritual where I hunt for bargains, spend time with friends, and get a cardio workout—shopping in places where you can find everything from antique chairs to metallic silver sequined jackets takes a lot of energy!

Whether you are driving around for Sunday garage sales or attending a church flea market, be aware of your arrival time. If you are keen on getting dibs on the selection, you'll want to be one of the first people there. But for the best deals, end-of-day is always better because most sellers want to unload whatever they can and are willing to bargain. Weather is another big factor in the price tag. As a shopper, bad weather works in your favor. Some flea markets are set up rain or shine, but who likes to stand in the rain? Use the sleet, snow, and rain as your bargaining chip.

HOW TO HAGGLE

It can be hard to get up the courage to bargain, but sellers are expecting it. So be confident and persistent as you follow these tips.

- Let a seller know if you saw something similar at another sale for a lower price. That's a great motivator for a drop in sales price.
- Offer to buy more than one for a discounted price. Instead of one bangle for twenty dollars, what about two bangles for thirty dollars?
- Take cash in five- and ten-dollar increments for easy bartering of prices down in increments of five.
- Always start lower than what you are willing to pay, to give the seller room to go up a little. Sometimes you have to walk away in order for them to budge on the sale. They never want to lose a paying customer to the next vendor.

Wholesale Districts

This is the place where the fashion industry gets merchandise to sell in stores. You can sometimes cut out the middleman and buy directly from the wholesale district! It's often a designated area with a few stores on one street, or several streets of stores that sell to vendors. The wholesale districts in major fashion cities like Los Angeles and New York City are larger than those in Washington, DC, and Atlanta. But all of them have great deals.

Some sellers are housed in showrooms in buildings like the California Market Center in downtown Los Angeles that grant access only to buyers, stylists, and boutique owners. If you have a wholesale or vendor's license, you can go anytime. Apply online for a business license—and while you're at it, see if your city's wholesale district has a website (many do). When visiting a store, ask if there is a minimum order. You can get accessories and costume jewelry in bulk, way below retail year-round, which is great if you're hosting an event and need fashion items for gift bags. Or, if all your friends love gold hoop earrings, you can buy a pack of twelve for ten bucks (cash talks louder than credit cards in this case) to give them away. Wholesale stores will sometimes sell single items to regular shoppers for a slightly higher price, and many are open to nonbusiness shoppers for specific hours and days every month. The best way to get in the know is to pay a visit to the district and talk to the owners.

Attention, Bargain Babes

Some cities like New York, Los Angeles, and Paris have shopping themed bus tours based on everything from movies like *Sex and the City* to bargain hunting. Most of the tours offer special discounts too! Google "shopping tours" the next time you are in a fashionable side of town to find a bonus on wheels.

Global Shopping

Every year a global trend surfaces, and some part of the world is deemed fashionable. This is usually a result of a creative development team's or a designer's traveling to some cool interesting place to find inspiration for a collection. Then the rest of us live vicariously by wearing expensive pieces from specialty stores where we'll pay more because it is a silk from China or beaded in Africa.

Find your own runway-worthy trends while on vacation. You can move past the souvenir shops and T-shirts that say "I Love Beijing." On my trip to Puerto Rico, I found the most darling cotton gauze ruffle peasant dresses with embroidered rosettes for my nieces. The same dresses were sold in high-end boutiques for close to $135 each, while I paid maybe $30 for both!

You don't need to go abroad to get great indigenous goods. You might find a Native American shop with great beaded pieces in Arizona or beautiful silk pajamas in San Francisco's Chinatown. In fact, you don't even need to leave home——check out your city's ethnic neighborhoods.

AROUND THE WORLD IN STYLE

If you have a trip planned to any of the places below, check out these local specialties.

- **Mexico and Puerto Rico:** peasant skirts, huarache sandals, cotton embroidered tunics, kaftans
- **Ethiopia:** caftans, yellow gold, beads
- **South and West Africa:** dashikis, African fabrics, oversize beads, wood bangles
- **India:** henna, saris, caftans, khussa shoes
- **Spain:** inexpensive leather summer sandals
- **Portugal:** beautiful terry cloth and embroidered tablecloths, dish towels, and other linens

Shopping Anywhere and Everywhere

Hey, why not? After diving into department stores, mastering the sample sale, and wheeling and dealing online, you still have more places to discover great bargains. Here are some random places to keep on your radar just in case you get an urge to keep the shopping celebration going.

HOSPITALS

They often have a thrift store or consignment shop for charity. After visiting the sick, stop by to cure your shopping addiction.

MUSEUMS

These stores have moved way past postcards and reproductions of Van Goghs and Picassos. You can find beautifully designed scarves inspired by the museum's collection and unique pieces of jewelry.

STUDENT STORES

Schools that have either really fashionable students or fashion majors tend to have great digs on sale in the student store. Check them out for pieces handmade by the next Michael Kors or *Project Runway* star.

COSTCO

After loading up on granola bars, baby wipes, and your favorite shampoo, check out the clothing section for items like socks, undies, and even designer jeans. The only problem you'll have is fitting all your goodies into your car and closet!

CHAIN DRUGSTORES

My cool cousin, Penny, turned me on to this tip. Drug stores are the place to find low-cost flip-flops, handy totes, and even colorful cotton summer sarongs and tunics.

TRUCK STOPS

They're the best place to find the perfect metallic aviator sunglasses (of which I own tons of pairs). Truck drivers need their sun protection, and fashion girls need style. Over and out!

AIRPORTS

On your next layover or during a delayed flight, instead of having a regretful carb fest in the food court, head into the themed discount stores where everything is only ten or twenty dollars for nifty finds. These stores are giving the higher end boutiques a run for their money. My mom and I stocked up on bright-hued scarves in tangerine, lime, and a beautiful grape (sounds like a fashionable fruit basket) in Virginia, for twenty dollars each.

Attention, Bargain Babes

At Hi-Fashion $5.99 stores in California, you can buy an entire outfit for less than six dollars. They don't offer the highest quality but are great for trends or fashion emergencies. Hi-Fashion even carries known labels like Express and Forever 21.

Navigating the Tricky Terrain of Sales Staff

We all have a salesperson horror story. A pushy store clerk who insists you look great in that purple ruffled taffeta number and practically holds you hostage in the dressing room. Or there's the person who refuses to make eye contact as you request a larger size. Stand up for your right to shop with dignity. In reality, most sales staff are nice and really do want to help. But I have a few methods to improve your customer relations, no matter whether you get someone as sweet as cherry pie or cold as Puff Daddy's icy diamonds. If at first some of these suggestions feel awkward, just keep trying and watch your circle of sales friends expand like crazy.

Salespeople have the power to help you get what you want—the best pieces in hard-to-find sizes, a sneak peak at the collections before they hit the sales floor, exclusive scoop on new deliveries, exact dates of markdowns, and more. All you have to do is be strategic. So let's call a truce and make those former enemies your newfound fashion friends. Here are my five surefire ways for dazzling all sales staff, snooty and sweet.

1. DRESS THE PART.

Fashion is about your appearance. Sure, that's shallow, but you need to learn how to work it in your favor. If you want to be taken seriously by the fashion industry, you must dress the part. Your goal is to look stylishly put together. Does this mean you have to shop in a Zac Posen couture gown and Harry Winston jewels? Uh, no— although it *would* be nice. Just look great for your shopping day. If you wear nothing else, make sure you carry a great bag and wear great shoes. This is the standard 365-day-a-year secret fashion rule. *Always have a good bag and shoes.* Healthy layers in your hair and a chip-free mani don't hurt either. Notice the way the salesgirls, valet guys, doorman, even the barista in the café respond to you when you're put together.

Your outerwear and accessories, such as coat and sunglasses, are just as important—if not more important—than what you wear underneath. If there is a good sale going on, I barely even bother taking off my sunglasses or coat when I step inside the store. For a guaranteed stylish outer layer, my vote goes to the three-quarter-length belted trench in khaki, black, or a bright bold color. There's something about a perfectly upright starched collar that screams, "I mean business!" A special ballet flat with decorative ornamentation or a comfy platform is the way to go (layer shoe pads under the entire sole with extra padding at the ball and heel to extend your comfy shopping hours).

If you have bought a piece from a store, or own any of the brands that they carry, it doesn't hurt to wear them. If you don't own any, no need to cancel your shopping trip.

It's one of those things that's great if you are able to do it, but won't make a huge world of difference if you can't.

2. DO YOUR HOMEWORK.

Many salesgirls in high-end boutiques and department stores are fashion fanatics. Show them that you are too! Before you go in, flip through a few magazines and fashion websites for a quick study session on current collections. You can drop knowing comments about the cut of a specific designer's pants or the hot new heel shape. Referring to designers by their first or last names only is pretty common for die-hard shoppers and fashion industry types. Christian Louboutin shoes are just Louboutins, and Stella McCartney is simply Stella. Check the style dictionary for the pronunciation of some of the tougher names since they can get tricky. Sales staff enjoy and value working with people who know what they like and what they are looking for. So don't be afraid to speak up. It actually makes their job easier.

3. BE STRATEGIC.

Are you a Barneys girl (i.e., are you a fan of obscure European labels and statement shoes) or a Saks fan (a new Tory Burch tunic or the latest Tracy Reese frock is your idea of a little slice of heaven) or bananas for Bergdorf (cashmere is your middle name and the Carolina Manolo Blahnik pump is your birth child)? If you pick a department store that suits your personal style, chances are you'll have more in common style-wise with the people who work there. I will never forget the time I took my twelve-year-old niece T'sai to Fred Segal in Santa Monica, where she didn't know whether to admire or run away from the salesguy with the wildly braided mohawk. Once you've identified the store and floor that has the clothes and accessories you want in your closet, pick a salesgirl to befriend.

4. LIGHTS, CAMERA, FASHION, CHARM!

Flashing your pearly whites will get you many privileges and perks. Find something nice to compliment your salesgirl on: her outfit, her necklace, or the store. Everyone appreciate praise. Always ask the name of the salesperson helping you and offer your own name. You are now on a first-name basis! Inquire how her day is going. If you had a previous conversation, mention that. Ask her about something that might trigger her memory about your last visit, like "Oh, how was your birthday party?" or "Did you guys ever get those jeans that I fell in love with in my size?"

Try your best to buy something from her, even if it's a small thing like tights or a pair of boycut undies or socks. Don't be a stalker, but do ask her what days she works so you can shop when she's on duty: "You're so nice; are you always here on Fridays?" When you go back, always ask to be helped by her, so you can work on building your relationship. Refer your friends to her and make sure they drop your name when shopping. Loyalty is big in retail, since a lot of salespeople work on commission and the competition can be fierce. Once you've established a rapport, you can bring up the subject of sales and markdown days. If you love a particular item, chances are good your salesperson will not only let you know when the item in question is going on sale but will call you in advance and put your size aside.

5. BE GRACIOUS.

Once you've acquired the bag, shoes, or dress of your dreams, send a handwritten thank-you note to the person who helped you, and perhaps to her manager. Yes, just like your grandmother taught you to do. When writing your note, make sure to reference what she helped you with. Thank her for sharing her great taste and amazing service. I know shop owners that like to see pictures from the event for which they helped the clients prepare. It's a job well done on their part! Always enclose your business card so the shop has your information. If you're extra grateful, send along a small token gift: a bouquet of pretty peonies or a box of chocolates for the team to share. You'll be etched in the salesperson's memory as a true VIP.

SHOP TALK WITH . . . **Danielle Rohani, manager of the L.A. boutique Madison, frequented by practically every stylist and celeb (Jennifer Lopez, Cindy Crawford, Reese Witherspoon, and Nicole Richie included)**

"I actually prefer to have a client book full of women who aren't famous and don't have personal stylists already making fashion decisions for them—it makes my job more interesting and exciting. It's pretty amazing when I can join a pair of Marni shoes with a customer who has been dreaming of them since she saw them in the pages of the September *Vogue.* You don't have to hire a stylist to re-create your look or update your wardrobe. Because we are in the stores every day, we really know how everything is fitting and what the season's best pieces are. We are a free resource available every day of the week!"

Phew! That was quite a shopping trip. I don't know if you are as exhausted as I am. Online, at the department stores, in the discount chains, around the wholesale district, and all over flea markets—there are wonderful stylish bargains to be found just about everywhere. It can really tire a girl out. But before you kick back and gaze lovingly at all your new and amazing outfits, there's still a whole other realm of the Bargain Babe lifestyle for you to conquer. I'm talking about selling. That's right, selling your stuff. *What does that have to do with shopping?* Absolutely everything. Unless you are Imelda Marcos, with enough closet space to house three thousand pairs of shoes, you are going to have to make some room for your new purchases. Plus, selling clothes you no longer wear is a terrific way to raise capital for future shopping excursions. See, it's all part of the circle of life. Now, let me show you how to unload those unwanted items for top dollar.

Selling 5 Yourself

Magazine editors, stylists, and other people who work in fashion can't possibly wear all the clothes they buy at sample sales or get as freebies. Some go to dear friends and some are donated to worthy causes. But let me tell you, a lot of it also gets resold. A girl's gotta eat. When there's a pair of Bottega Veneta boots that retail for a thousand dollars sitting in their original tissue paper in the closet, even the most fashionable types aren't above putting them on eBay or bringing them to a consignment shop for some cold hard cash.

If it's good enough for them, it should be good enough for you too. Most likely you have some costly items sitting in your closet that never get use. Did your ex-boyfriend try to impress you with a fancy sweater from Saks, but now just looking at it makes you spit fire? Toss it in your Sell Bag. If you're not wearing it and are never going to wear it again, I say sell it and get something you really want with the cash. Always make sure items are in good condition. High-end popular designer items are sometimes pardoned for slight wear and tear, but the value of your return will depreciate. Classic high-end designer pieces like Chanel and Hermès always have a good chance of being purchased. The same is true of super-trendy pieces that have received recent press or news. Pieces with original tags are always a nice plus. You worked hard shopping for those clothes. Now it's time for a little payback.

Consignment Sales

When I lived in Brooklyn and could persuade my buddy Erica to let me borrow her rust-colored Nissan with the primer-colored polka dots, I would load it down with my cast-offs and head to a consignment shop called Beacon's Closet. I would enter with a heap of clothes and leave with a pocket filled with cash. Every city, mini or massive, has its own version of Beacon's Closet. Check out the Appendix for some in your neck of the woods. At resale stores like Beacon's, they will offer you cash (usually a percentage of the estimated total value of your goods) or a higher-value store credit. Whether you walk away with green bills or a cute green skirt, you win.

Before you cart your stuff to the local consignment shop, consider where you live and what's a hot commodity. If you're selling somewhere like New York City, designers like Phillip Lim and Marc Jacobs are always going to rule. If you are selling in a smaller town without much local shopping, they may be more willing to buy trendy items from stores like H&M and Forever 21. Sell season-appropriate items like sandals in the spring and summer, and fur coats and wool skirts in the fall and winter.

Gather items that you no longer want and place them in your Sell Bag. Oversize Ziploc bags are perfect for this. Set a personal goal of filling two or three bags of stuff before you go. It's better to have options, as you never know what a shop will actually accept until you arrive. It's a good idea to have your pieces freshly laundered, pressed, or dry-cleaned to make the best impression possible. Drop off your merchandise at the store for review from the buyer. On busier days like Saturdays and Sundays, retailers will call you back when your assessment is complete. Many will call you later that same day, though busier stores may not be able to get back to you for two to seven days after you drop off. During slower times, like weekday mornings, they will usually give you an on-the-spot assessment.

You get to choose between Door Number One (cash) or Door Number Two (store credit). The better stores will offer you an itemized list of how much they want to pay for each item. Some stores offer to sell the items for you, and then you get a percentage once it actually sells. If it does not sell within their allotted time, usually two to three months, you go pick your stuff up and try again elsewhere. You need a tough skin because consignment shop buyers couldn't care less about the sentimental value of an item or how much you slaved to save to buy it. So hold the tears.

If you think your merchandise is high quality and you're not wild about the consignment shops in your area, it can be worth taking a road trip to better stores in order to get the best cash value. Stores like Buffalo Exchange (which is a countrywide chain) and Beacon's have a mix of vintage/retro and trendy pieces, as opposed to stores like Fisch for the Hip in Manhattan's trendy Chelsea that focus mostly on designer labels. Do your research on the stores in advance, so you're aware of what they're currently looking for. A simple call is all it takes. Stores will have seasonal specifics that they are searching for based on their customers' demographic. Always be aware of what other sellers are selling. If the store does not want to buy their pieces, you might! You can always do a sidewalk trade with something that you have in your Sell Bag. It will be even better than that brown bag lunch swapping you used to do back in grade school.

Best Months to Sell

March: Fashion magazines come out with their spring trend issues.

May: The sun starts to peek out and people wake up from their winter comas.

September: Fashion magazines come out with their fall trend issues.

November: Consumers, who like to impress and avoid tragic lines, begin holiday shopping.

Labels that Sell Fast Everywhere

- Louis Vuitton
- Prada
- Chanel
- Hermès
- Gucci
- Fendi

Online Sales

What if I told you that you could start a fashion boutique with big names, big designs, and big style and not pay a dime of rent? No, I am not suggesting you sell your clothes from the back of your car. All you need for this store is a steady hand for snapping pix, an eye for what people are buying, and a working computer. I am talking about a virtual fashion boutique.

Online selling is a painless way to make money from your style sense. Amazon, Craigslist, and eBay have created a universe for selling all things fashion. If you've got something to sell, very likely there is a person surfing the web who would be interested in purchasing it.

There are even a few unexpected items you may have around that can bring in extra bucks:

- Extra-special buttons from the inside of a garment, especially versions with a designer logo
- Discontinued beauty products
- Designer packaging such as shoe bags, shoe boxes, shopping bags, garment bags, tissue paper
- Buzz items that a celebrity was recently photographed wearing
- Empty perfume bottles
- Designer hangers
- Designer sunglasses cases
- Parts from broken items such as sunglasses, or hardware from bags and shoes

When it comes to online selling, it's important to start off on the right foot. Bad reviews can cost you. Here are some pointers on prepping for the opening of the doors to your cyber store.

BE HONEST

Tell the absolute truth, the whole truth, and nothing but the truth about what you are selling, how much it is worth, and why you are selling it. Shoppers will appreciate your honesty. Attaching links to the item with the original retail value is a great idea. It gives shoppers a sense of security that they are buying a recognizable brand and, most important, are getting a great deal. Don't ever give false information to boost your sales, as you can get reported and penalized.

ACCOUNTS ARE US

Open an account with a website that allows you to sell merchandise. If you prefer selling to local shoppers, go with Craigslist, since most people shopping are driving-distance away. Craigslist is categorized by city and state, making it easy for shoppers to search within their areas, and allowing them to drive to pick up a purchase rather than have it shipped. Amazon and eBay are terrific if you want to reach a larger audience and don't mind shipping outside of your area. You can charge for shipping and handling charges, so don't worry about them coming out of your pocket. If you are flexible, you can open an account with all three. Some areas even have a neighborhood blog and a social network where residents can post news and items for sale.

GET DETAIL-ORIENTED

Take detailed pictures of your items. Zoom in and capture the item from every single angle, both on the interior and exterior. Also take a full shot of the complete item, avoiding distracting elements in the background. You can even take images of it displayed on a mannequin. Make sure the picture is clear and reads true to the actual item. Every little detail counts, from the zipper on a bag to the scuffs on the heel of a pump. When you don't show the true visual of the item, you risk more bad reviews and returns from shoppers who discover unexpected surprises.

BE RESPONSIVE

It is important to leave a reliable source of contact information, such as an e-mail address that the site provides or your phone number. Once you share your information, be prepared to answer questions in a timely manner. Many people are inquiring as they comparison shop, so you may have a chance at beating your competition with your helpful and speedy responses. And please be gracious. If you listed an item as selling for a hundred dollars, and they ask how much is it, don't say, "A hundred, idiot." Customer service still stands in an online store.

BE REAL

Give a realistic time frame so they know when to expect their package. If you say you are sending the purchased item out, send it. Don't leave your customer waiting for that special delivery longer than you promised. That's another reputation ruiner.

GIVE UP THE GOOD STUFF

Although you can sell any- and everything online, you still want to have pride in your merchandise. If a silk blouse has a not-so-fresh underarm stench, then launder it in advance. It's okay to sell used merchandise, as long as it is still wearable. Imagine your best friend is your customer. Would she bid eagerly on the item or quickly click onto something else? Sell good-looking stuff that you think others might want to wear too.

GET CREATIVE

Set up a nice environment or backdrop for selling items. You can do easy things like taking a bright-colored solid gift bag or piece of fabric and photographing silver bangles on top of it. Try setting up a pseudo studio for your still-life shots. If you are selling clothing, avoid photographing it on person, as this may distract shoppers. People will judge your item based on your model and not the actual garment. A neutral canvas like a mannequin, a rolling rack, or even a tabletop is better. Make sure items stand out from the backdrop. Look at *InStyle*'s Instant Style section. It is a great example of photographs of clothes off the body that have shape and depth.

DIRECT DEPOSIT

Set up a PayPal account and allow shoppers to pay directly to the account. Most people will not feel comfortable giving their AmEx or checking account and routing number to a stranger, and this ensures both you and the shopper are protected. The money paid to your PayPal account goes directly into your bank account.

PRICE IT RIGHT

Online shoppers usually have one of two goals: locating a good deal or a hard-to-find-item. How you price things is a personal choice, but checking the online competition and the going price in stores should guide your decision.

Attention, Bargain Babes

There are agencies and stores that will sell your stuff for you, but they charge a fee. If you've got the time, take a page from their books and start your own business as an eBay seller for others. Charge a lower flat rate to take items, and then receive a commission from all the sales. Not everyone has the time to go through the motions of taking pictures, posting, and responding to inquiries, but many would love to have someone help them out.

SHOP TALK WITH . . . **Constance White,**
eBay's style director

How can shoppers get the most out of eBay?

Shop by brand. Don't just randomly search for something like "leggings." It would be much better to search for "Vera Wang leggings." Also shop by specifics, like the design of an item, its color, length, and anything else descriptive. This will help you narrow down your search. Be very specific in terms of price range that you are open to paying. If looking for a new bag designer, put in the price range that you're looking for.

How can you avoid buying knockoffs?

EBay encourages shoppers to check sellers' ratings. Shop with sellers with at least a 94 percent rating. Counterfeits are a big no-no and can be easily identified if you search for the red flags. Look out for key words like "resembles" or "looks like" if it is referring to a designer piece. Seek realistic prices, and beware if it seems too good to be true. In general, you should buy from sellers that offer returns.

Is there a specific technique to winning auctions?

Check when the auction is scheduled to end. There is even software available that will watch your auction bid for you on eBay if you don't have the time. EBay has millions of listings daily, and the activity, like with malls, increases on the weekends and during the end of an auction. These are also great times to score a good deal.

How can newcomers to eBay become great sellers?

Always check prices in the brick and mortar stores first. Offer as much detailed information as possible, and be completely honest about the sizing. If it is a 41 but fits a size 8, share that. If it fits a slim waist and longer legs, then share that. Be really honest and helpful when you sell.

Street Selling

One deserted holiday weekend, my friend Love and I decided on a whim to have a sidewalk sale outside our

Brooklyn apartment. "Sale" is a generous term. It was more like a pile of clothes, shoes, and whatever else we were over at the time thrown on the corner. Our apartment sat atop a tire shop and was the absolute worst place to have a sale. We didn't have any signs directing people to our sale, and we didn't even stick around! We peeked out of the window sporadically to see if we saw any potential shoppers. "Hey, you should get that," we yelled down. I think we scared more people than we attracted. We ended up begging people to take the stuff for free.

Don't make the same mistakes my roommate and I did. If you are going to hold a sidewalk, stoop, or lawn sale, put as much care and thought into it as you would if you were opening a store. Here are a few things to keep in mind.

- You want to choose a non-holiday weekend when more residents will likely be in town. Avoid Memorial Day, Fourth of July, and Labor Day weekends.
- Check your local city or town paper for scheduling conflicts. You want to avoid major events like free concerts and family fests that can potentially take away from your expected crowd.
- Watch the weather report a week in advance. Rain

will put a major damper on your sale, so consider re-scheduling in even the threat of bad weather.

- If you know someone who lives in a busy neighborhood with lots of foot traffic, see if you can have the sale outside his or her house.

PREP STEPS

I like to compare getting ready for a sale to what brands do when they're prepping for a fashion trade show. The sales team pretties up their space just like a chic showroom. Some of the really fanciful booths have yummy candies and treats, like cookies or crudités. Set up your sale the same way and make everything as attractive as possible. You can use old sarongs, or brightly colored co-ordinating sheets, or even a pretty blanket as the center selling backdrop. This is your boutique, and you want to sell everything because packing up is never much fun.

Advertise Like Crazy

Place an ad with the local paper a week in advance of your sale, and put flyers up around the neighborhood on the Thursday and Friday beforehand. Have someone pass more flyers out early Saturday. Send a quick Evite to friends and neighbors.

Clean Up Your Act

Prep everything two nights before by washing, shaking out, polishing, and anything else in your power to make your merchandise look appealing. There is nothing worse than a funk-infested sweater. Remember, this will represent your style and charm.

Supply and Demand

Get all your supplies in advance, including:

- Lawn chairs (leave the rusty ones in the backyard and bring out the nicer patio chairs).
- Music you and your shoppers will enjoy. Nothing too aggressive or random that will disturb the neighbors.
- Packing supplies such as bags, ribbon, tissue paper, or newspaper to wrap delicates.
- Rolling rack for hanging items.
- Blankets, fabric, and sheets on which to display items.
- Balloons and bold attention-getters like Chinese paper lanterns in bright colors.
- Tags for style notes such as "Look like Sharon Stone in *Basic Instinct* for 25 cents."

- Cute shoulder purse for change. I *beg* you to forgo the awful and infamous fanny pack.

Recruit Friends to Sell

If you would like to have a joint sale, call on your buds who are semiorganized and see if they have items to bring over to sell.

Have a Plan for the Lonely Leftovers

Although I'm confident that your sale will be fantastic and the shoppers will be fighting over every last piece, you may be left with a few unclaimed items. Before you even begin your sale, decide whether you want to donate what's left, keep it for another weekend sale (which you should advertise at your sale), organize a free clothing swap with friends, or sell it to a resale or consignment shop. In the last hour of your sale, start to pull out your packing materials, bags, boxes, or whatever else you unpacked from. For items being donated, arrange for them to be picked up the same day, or drop them off yourself. But don't make the mistake of waiting twenty-four hours, or those leftovers will likely land back in your closet.

Tips for Selling at Large Flea Markets and Public Sidewalk Sales

- Fees for space rentals at flea markets can range from $35 to $300, so check for the best spot for the best value.
- Go a few times in advance to scout where the most foot traffic seems to be.
- Some markets are on a first-come first-serve basis, so arrive early in order to claim a good spot near the entrance, on the route to the food, or in other high-traffic areas.
- Invite friends or family to partner with you in order to have a bigger and more appealing sale. You will also be able to split the costs of space rental fees, etc.

Isn't it amazing how a dress you are totally over, or maybe never really loved in the first place, can be someone else's fashion fantasy? One woman's castoffs are another woman's new outfit. Perhaps you discovered that fact with a killer garage sale where all the neighbors were snatching up stuff from the back of your closet. Or your eBay store is buzzing with folks bidding on the scarf collection you had hiding under your bed. Whatever your mode of selling, the outcome is the same: You've now found a little extra cash in your pocket. And I'm going to help you make the most of that money with—what else—more shopping! In the next chapter, we are going to take it to the next level and learn how to shop like the pros.

6 Tricks of the Trade

During my magazine days, both at *Glamour* and at *In-Style*, a really fun part of my job was working on our annual summer denim issue. One very important step was to make the "requests"—a fashion term for calling publicists and asking them to send in samples of their clients' wares. In this case it was tons and tons and more tons of jeans. We received every kind of denim, from Mossimo for Target to See by Chloé. Walking down the long halls lined with over five hundred pairs of jeans, skirts, jackets, and anything else ever created with denim (rinsed, distressed, white, whatever), I felt like I was in a never-ending Divine Denim Dream. During the editing process, we went through every pair to find the ones that worked for different budgets and body types, and a special pair for the celebrity cover photo shoot.

After an intense process like that, your eye really starts to notice the fine details of what makes each pair of jeans special (or in some cases, not so special!). If you expand that editing process into every aspect of shopping, you'll be a Never Pay Retail Again Honors Fashion Graduate Extraordinaire. Working for a great fashion magazine heightens your senses so that you can smell quality a mile away. You also learn to identify the definitely-not-making-the-cut piece. I have something called Cheap-Dar: I can instantly identify an item that has a high price tag but simply isn't worth it, or a low-end piece that is super inexpensive and really, really well made. Although they are important factors, the price or name of a brand is not the qualifying factor. I've been trained to identify the crème de la crème in every genre of labels, from the highest of the high-end to the lowest-priced brands—and now I want to pass this knowledge on to you. I want all women to shop with an editor's eye.

So listen up, because this is going to be the best lesson that you never learned in school. As you start to shop like an editor, you will set standards for yourself. You won't just buy something because "it's only ten bucks," and you won't assume that it is immaculately made and stylish simply because it has a high price tag. You will be able to spot an amazing diamond in the rough, a keeper that works for your wardrobe. The item could be something to which most would not even give the time of day, maybe a designer markdown in a discount store hidden on a crowded clearance rack, or a top thrown on a table at a church garage sale for fifty cents. You will always know how to look like a million bucks, even if you spent only fifteen!

The Inspection

By understanding what goes into a quality bag, shoe, or dress, whether in the poshest boutique or a suburban flea market, you will have a wardrobe made up of clothes you love to wear and not just pieces that take up good closet space. The most accurate way to evaluate why you should buy some items and pass on others is to give them the "inspection."

No matter the garment or accessory, your inspection checklist should include the following:

1. Fabric or material
2. Colors and prints
3. Construction and shape
4. Detailing

Always take note of these elements, no matter where you shop. It's the checklist, not the price tag, that's key. Once you complete your checklist, you'll understand why some celebs can look so darn cute in a simple pair of jeans and a T-shirt.

FABRIC

The actual fabric or material that your clothes are made of can make a world of difference when it comes to how they fit and feel on your body. If you like the way a piece of clothing feels, take a peek at the tag to familiarize yourself with what it's made of. Look for similar materials in other pieces that you shop for. Some of my favorites include two-ply cashmeres that are always yummy on the skin; matte jersey, which makes everyone's body feel like a trillion bucks; liposuction-mimicking Lycra; or a good, old-fashioned easy-to-wash, baby-soft cotton.

FABRICS 101

Apply these fabric tips when shopping to save both money and the agony of unexpected returns.

- **Lace:** A very delicate, ornamental fabric that can be extremely costly to produce, especially when made by hand. Beware of rough, scratchy varieties that do more harm than good.
- **Satin:** When structured well and of good quality, it can look lovely. But beware of wrinkles, a common nightmare with this tricky fabric.
- **Knits:** High-end knits will feel smooth and resist pilling (forming little balls) longer than lower-quality knits. The finer the knit, the more easily they can tear and snag.
- **Cotton:** The fabric of our lives has great durability and is ideal in a perfect T-shirt or summer dress. Make sure it feels good against the skin and has excellent resilience, which means the item goes back to its original shape after being stretched.
- **Cashmere:** Made from the hair of the cashmere goat, this is one of the warmest, softest wools around. There are many grades of cashmere available on the market now, with the finest made from the beard of the goat. The higher the quality, the higher the price.
- **Stretch:** High-quality stretch fabrics should have great flexibility and resilience and not lose their shape too quickly.

- **Velvet:** Beware of cheap, bulky-looking velvets. High-quality velvet should be smooth and baby soft with a nice, light weight.

- **Leather and suede:** Cheap skins often have a strong smell, while more expensive ones do not. Leather should be as smooth as butter. Watch out for suede that does not have a fine grain and appears patchy in color.

- **Skins:** Beware of imitators that are printed or embossed to look like python or crocodile. Moc croc and embossed fabrics should be much lower in price than genuine skins. The more exotic the skin and unique its color and finish, the more expensive it will be.

- **Jersey:** A good-quality jersey will swing and flow with your walk, not droop and sag. The classic Diane von Furstenberg wrap dress is constructed from matte jersey, one of the most flattering fabrics a girl can wear.

- **Polyester:** A retro fabric that's been modernized, poly can perform surprisingly well in garment construction. Wear it in small doses, though, so you don't look too seventies or *Boogie Nights* or die from a sweat rash (polyester is not traditionally a breathable fabric like cotton).

- **Denim:** It can be washed, distressed, dyed, torn, and ripped apart, all to create a unique design. The treatments on denim can boost the price. Beware of low-quality versions that can look and feel rough.

- **Silk:** An expensive, soft, lustrous fiber obtained from the cocoon of the

(continued)

silkworm, silk is prevalent in Asia. There are great imitation silks such as viscose that look similar but cost a lot less.

- **Linen:** A natural fabric woven from flax yarns, linen should have a smooth surface and not be scratchy. Linen wrinkles easily, but the wrinkles should smooth out once you've hung up the garment, especially in a hot, steamy room (I like to steam linen in the bathroom while I shower).

- **Lycra:** This fabric changed the way clothes fit women of all shapes and sizes (think of the way a pair of jeans with just 1 or 2 percent Lycra feels). It also does wonders for figure enhancing. Try Lycra for a tummy-tucking undergarment!

COLORS AND PRINTS

Wearing colors and prints (including metallic fabrics like silver, bronze, and gold) is an amazing way to bring personality and life to your wardrobe. Always make sure that the dyes are well saturated and vivid in the piece. You need to be especially careful with black. If a black garment appears chalky or slightly faded, and that's not an intentional part of the distressed finish, it's a sign that it will likely lose even more color. When it comes to color, prints, metallics, and even pastels, boldness is imperative.

The best way to identify great prints is to study designers known for them, such as Tracy Reese, Missoni, Milly, and Tory Burch. They make amazing printed pieces, which can serve as the gold standard for print quality. Check the fabric closely to see whether the pattern was printed on or woven into the garment—if the threads of the garment match the colors in the print, on both sides of the garment, that means that the piece was woven and is therefore of better quality. If the threads of the fabric on one side of the garment are lighter in color than the other side, that means the fabric was printed.

SHOP TALK WITH . . . **Tracy Reese,**
fashion designer

"You can have a great print, but if the material itself is cheap or flimsy, it will shine through no matter how stunning the print may be. The pattern lining up at the seams is another telltale sign of a quality print."

Color Check

These fashion-savvy hues will look great year after year:

- **Jewel tones:** rich burgundies and deep reds, bright greens and blues, and purples that pop
- **Pastels and sorbet colors:** baby pink, lavender, light blue, seafoam green, and pale yellow
- **Neutrals:** camel, caramel, heather gray, charcoal gray, espresso brown, creme, and white
- **Metallics:** gold, bronze, and silver
- **Black**

Pretty in Prints

These classics done in the right fabric work no matter the outfit or season:

- Florals
- Stripes and pinstripes
- Graphic prints
- Ethnic prints
- Animal prints

CONSTRUCTION AND SHAPE

When items look similar but fit differently, there are generally two main reasons behind the disparity: (1) the garment's fabric, or (2) the way it is constructed. A well-made garment will last you a lifetime, because a well-constructed piece made from a quality fabric won't lose its shape from your taking it on and off.

That's true even with a T-shirt. My mom had a drawer full of T-shirts in every color and shape. But one thing was missing: a good fit. They were thick and high-necked and did not do her body justice. Upon my urging, she did a quick upgrade to better T-shirts with Lycra (your body lifesaver) from Banana Republic. Sure enough, she felt like a new woman. Brands and stores like J.Crew, American Apparel, Gap, and Banana Republic make amazing T-shirts that fit so well and are equally well priced.

When shopping, be mindful of the way different designers size their items. As a reminder, every brand cuts a little differently, and not every size-eight dress fits every size-eight woman. You may be a size six at the Gap, and a size ten in Dolce & Gabbana. You have to try different brands until you find the ones that work best for your specific body type. Traditionally, more mainstream American store brands like Banana Republic and Old Navy will be cut more generously than Italian, French, and British designers. Go U.S.A.! Gotta love it when labels are kind!

WELL BUILT

Here are the key elements that contribute to the construction and shape of an item.

Fit: Always check the way a garment falls on your body. It should not pucker or strain at the seams.

Design Details: Added perks like ruching, pintucking, pleating, shirring, and smocking mean that a garment was labor intensive. When properly executed, these details add to the value of a piece.

Seams, Hems, and Darts: Always check that your seams are tightly and evenly sewn and not crooked. Hems should not be obvious—you should not be able to see where the fabric was folded over on the underside. Darts should be flat and unnoticeable.

Topstitching: Check that there are no missing or skipped stitches and that the thread matches the color of the garment, unless it's meant to contrast.

Pockets: These should always lie flat and be very discreet. Bulky pockets take away from the design and visually add pounds.

Inside Finishing and Lining: Always check a garment's selvage on the inside, which is the multiple loop stitching on the edge of the fabric. It should be tightly in place. The lining should be either silk or something similarly smooth, and should lie evenly and close to the garment.

Zippers and Closures: These should fit in with the overall look of the garment and should coordinate in terms of color, size, and style. Always check for loose stitching.

DETAILING

The details of a garment are as important as the overall design. As small as they are, they can make a big statement. Buttons, patches, crystals, paillettes, sequins, and other embellishments attached to a garment are known collectively as "notions." They enhance a piece's quality and style. They also tell you how much additional work went into making the piece, and how design-driven the brand is (a brand that specializes in basic standard solid T-shirts is not going to be as design-driven as one that makes highly embellished T-shirts and blouses). Always check that notions are securely attached. If you love the garment and it's on sale but the notions are hanging by a thread, why not secure them yourself at home? I am so happy my mom encouraged me to learn to sew as a teen. Everyone who loves clothes should at least take a beginners' class. You learn how to fix and embellish great pieces, instantly becoming your own designer! And while you're at it, learn to identify a high-quality notion in stores and in sewing shops.

IT'S IN THE DETAILS

If you get the notion, check out these elements that signal the quality of a garment.

Buttons: Really special pieces can have buttons that are covered in the same fabric as the garment, or buttons in unique shapes, sizes, and colors. Buttons can be made of unusual materials such as rhinestones or crystal. Flat plastic buttons with two to four holes are usually the least expensive to produce.

Sequins: These flat shiny babies, also known as paillettes, can make the dullest items shine like a fresh manicure with three layers of glossy Sally Hansen topcoat. The best sequins are strikingly shiny and reflect the light.

Crystal Beading: This can range from a few scattered crystals to a huge overlay that makes a striking (and heavy) fashion statement. High-quality stones have weight and depth. Swarovski crystals have by far the best shine.

Rivets and Studs: They should be firmly attached and have a fluid color or finish, with no spotting or fading.

Trim: Check for specialty trim in lace, eyelet, grosgrain, fur, or anything that is out of the ordinary.

The Surprise Element: Always look for unexpected details—like a dress with gold lamé cording shoulder straps instead of ordinary fabric ones, or a black blazer with a flash of hot pink lining that will garner you plenty of compliments.

Inspection Assignment

It's awesome when you can perform an inspection at two stores with different price points. You'll be shocked by what you find! Select two stores, one a more high-end department store or specialty boutique, the other a lower-priced mass retailer—say, Saks Fifth Avenue vs. Target. Try to find similar items in both stores—check for a basic navy suit in Saks and a basic navy suit in Target. As you look around and try on the pieces, go through your inspection checklist. You might discover that the suit in Target has much better construction than the one in the higher-end store.

How to Tell Your Fashion Future

Besides my birthday in January, two of my favorite times of the year fall around February and September. These are the destination months for New York Fashion Week—the holy time of style. September is always my favorite fashion week month because the temperatures haven't dropped yet, so you don't have to bundle up with coats and hats just to go to shows, as you do in February. All the better for checking out what the world's biggest fashion moguls are wearing that season. Air kisses, hugs, and lots of fashion love are exchanged as editors, stylists, buyers, celebs, and designers gather together for the ultimate fashion preview of what's to come for the upcoming season. The cool parties, swag bags, and people-watching are priceless, but the key reason for attending shows is to be on the front lines of what will be the season's hottest trends in hues, silhouettes, and fabrics.

As the fashion gurus go from show to show, they take notes as to what they think the public will love best. Then they come together with their teams for a trend forecasting powwow. They discuss what looks were consistent from collection to collection, what was unusual, and what was a major standout. Since all of the shows take place three to six months before the clothes hit the stores, all buying, fashion stories, and trend forecasting for the upcoming season is planned about that much time in advance. So if you want to know what you will be wearing next season, ditch the psychic hotline and go the guaranteed route. Trend forecast like the pros. You'll be able to start shopping in advance, well before the competition. And you'll broaden your shopping horizons to include consignment shops and vintage stores, both of which are excellent places to shop off-season for similar styles that will eventually hit the racks at department stores and boutiques. You will be shocked to discover how many things you already have in your very own closet that are deemed as spring's or fall's Must-Have Item. Here's how you can peer into your very own fashion crystal ball to find the styles everyone will soon be desiring.

READ LIKE THE *VOGUE* GIRLS

There are special industry magazines and daily periodicals like *Women's Wear Daily* that share insider information on what will be major for accessories, clothing, and even beauty trends for the next one to two seasons

to come. You can also check any of the *Collezioni* magazines like *Uomo, Accessori, Trends,* and *Bambini.* They
are chock full of the ultimate trend forecasting visuals
from color, to shape, to textures and fabrics. Focus on
trend reports in your favorite magazines during March
for spring/summer trends, and September for fall/win-
ter trends.

GO TO FASHION WEEK

You can get a front-row seat to major designer fashion
shows in New York City, Paris, Milan, and London without disguising yourself as stylist-to-the-stars Rachel Zoe.
Style.com and Elle.com feature complete coverage of all
the hottest shows, as well as bios of the designers and
photos of the celebrities who attended their shows. And
during Fashion Week, these sites are updated *by the min-
ute,* so you'll feel like you're right there with the models,
designers, celebs, and paparazzi. These sites are the exact
same ones that stylists use to choose gowns for celebs attending the Academy Awards and the Golden Globes.
Fashion editors also consult these sites before selecting
the clothes for celebrity cover shoots. They are free to
anyone with an Internet connection! Once you see styles

that you like, you'll be inspired to crank up your radar for the best looks from the upcoming fashion season.

FORGET THE FUTURE AND STICK TO THE CLASSICS

Take an extra dose of gingko and eat plenty of brain food, because you'll need to remember all of your wardrobe season staples—the ones you've never been able to live without. If you have been loyal to these styles, you can go ahead and stamp them as your personal wardrobe essentials that contribute to your signature style. Thanks to my Bicoastal Babe life, I cannot function without my Jackie O glasses and a great bright scarf, which are essential for the climate change from L.A. to New York. Luckily, Jackie O glasses seem to be "in" every summer. Though it sounds like a contradiction, there are classic trends, ones that are guaranteed to be in demand not just for the season, but for the same season next year! Any season where there is sun, summer or fall, I know just where to look in my sunglasses drawer for those fun, girly glasses. Think back on what works for you and what still might be hiding in your closet, check out the Internet sites and the mags, and trend forecast away on what might be a classic that's part of your own signature style.

CLASSICS FOR ALL SEASONS

You'll get your money's worth with these timeless staples.

Spring

- *Belted trench coats:* This belted beauty has been passed down through the style generations, and thanks to the Burberry inspiration, it can be found in all stores, for all price points.
- *Printed floral skirts:* Florals are debuted every spring, sometimes in bold prints and other times in sweeter delicate blooms, but spring has never gone without flowers in the garden or florals on the runway.
- *Colored tanks:* A simple colored tank has the ability to brighten spring neutrals like khaki and gray.

Consistent spring colors: sorbet hues like pinks, apple green, and cantaloupe

Summer

- *Flat special sandals:* Sexy heels are amazing, but being sexy, stylish, and comfortable is as amazing as fat-free New York cheesecake. Summer days and nights will forever be filled with special sandals, especially for the urban dwellers who like to take strolls in the city streets without aching toes.

- *Espadrilles:* From the French Riviera to backyard BBQs, the espadrille has taken center stage year after year.
- *White jeans:* A summer alternative to darker hues, they look amazing with bright tunics and tanks.
- *Oversize Jackie O shades in black or tortoise:* Anything that Jackie O wore has an infinite stamp of classic chic. Her oversize shades, coined "Jackie O glasses," will be around as long as style mavens walk the earth.

Consistent summer colors: white and bright citrus hues

Fall

- *Colored coats:* Winter woes are immediately brightened when you see a confident beauty strutting in a great bold-colored coat. They are like a breath of fresh air amid the many dark hues.
- *Nude/neutral coats:* This is a great canvas for winter days and nights to pair with monotone looks or brightly colored bags.
- *Wool menswear trousers:* The heavy wool fabric will keep your legs warm without having to wear stockings or tights underneath.
- *Flat riding boots:* The riding boot is the fall version of the special sandal. They are easy on the toes, eyes, and wallet. (continued)

- *Chunky cable-knit sweaters in creme:* These are the perfect combination of comfort, luxury, and warmth.

Consistent fall colors: gray, chocolate, creme, and nude caramel

Winter

- *Fur accessories:* If winter weather includes snow and wind, fur—both real and faux—will remain constant. Stylish and functional, accessories such as scarves or cuffs are great for those of us who can't afford a full-length mink.
- *Jewel-tone velvet blazers:* Channeling holiday ornaments, the jewel-tone velvet blazer is a festive option that will sparkle for parties and celebratory soirées.
- *Cocktail dresses:* Holidays call for numerous celebrations, sometimes even back to back. Christmas, New Year's, office annuals, and more always call for a sexy cocktail getup.
- *Knit dresses:* The knit dress, though underrated, is an option that warms tushes and wows admirers.
- *Opaque tights:* They are the best way to warm up next to sipping hot chocolate by the fire.

Consistent winter colors: jewel tones and metallics

Resort*

- *Printed tunics and cover-ups:* Very versatile, these pieces can be worn as tops or cover-ups for your swimsuit.

- *Sexy one-piece swimsuits:* The one-piece has often gotten a bad rap, but sexy versions reign supreme with women who are not crazy about showing off their abs.

- *Triangle two-piece bikinis with tie bottoms:* The classic bikini shape can be worn on many body types, and every season is debuted in amazing prints, solids, and metallics.

- *Oversize sun hats:* UV rays have never been the most attractive accessory. For extra protection, the sun hat is the best option.

- *Oversize straw bags:* Vacations call for poolside entertainment . . . and supplies. The tote can fit your towel, iPod, summer reading picks, SPF, and more.

Consistent resort colors: candy-colored hues and brights

---

*The resort season is when designers release pieces that are not weather appropriate to wear during the winter months, but great for a sunny weekend away in a tropical climate.

Closet Makeover

The term "bargain" can mean a zillion different things. For women who are used to buying Oscar de la Renta at full price retail, five hundred dollars for a silk full skirt is the ultimate steal! On the other side of the shopping road are the gals who have never spent more than a hundred dollars on any item. And we have all been there, when our shopping budget is depleted and the only bargain that will satisfy us is "free ninety-nine," as one of my besties, Erica says.

But I'm about to reveal a sweet little secret. The pieces in your closet, the ones you already *paid* for, hold a wealth of untapped fashion options. And they're free! *Not my closet*, you are thinking. Well, if my research is correct, you probably have a lot of fabulous finds hidden in the dark corners of the closet, waiting to be pulled out to revamp your style. See, I conducted an unscientific sampling of girls on the street in New York and L.A., and my research shows that more than 80 percent of women should receive style citations for being repeat clothes-in-my-closet offenders. They reach for the same items over and over—the infamous Saturday jeans and shapeless tee, a shift dress and cropped cardigan, or the weekly heather gray pantsuit with go-to striped oxford. Cue the yawns!

If you thoroughly went through your entire wardrobe, you may be pretty surprised at how many pieces in your closet have never even been worn. The majority of the gals I surveyed even had items with the price tags still attached! So, what's the solution? Shop less? Heavens no! Give yourself a closet makeover. Most people get into a fashion rut because they can't actually see most of the clothes in their closet. Stuff is usually totally disorganized and jammed into every nook and cranny.

Stylists and editors treat their closets like sanctuaries (well, not all of them), often devoting an extra little room to house their vast collections. They know the importance of being able to look over all your clothes to find new and interesting combinations. By reorganizing a messy closet, you will extend your wardrobe two- or threefold. Not only will you save money when you realize you already have fall's new must-have item in two colors, but you will also save time getting dressed.

INSIDE THE IDEAL CLOSET

Hanging Items

- First organize by silhouette and shape: For example, hang all your skirts in one section, followed by pants, followed by blouses, etc.

- Then organize by color, based on the most prominent: In your skirt section, hang all the black skirts together, then the brown ones, tan, white, yellow, pink, red, green, blue, purple, yellow, and prints. Repeat this color order for the rest of your silhouettes and shapes.

- Hang all your hangers facing the same way: Aim to keep them the same way as you shop your closet. It will make creating outfits easier and faster.

- Invest in good-quality hangers: Purchase thin, heavy-duty hangers with protective material. They save a lot of space in tiny closets!

Folded Items

- Set up your folded items in stacks, with the most prominent details facing upward.

- All jeans should be folded in half, then two short folds with detailed pocket exposed.

Shoes

- If you don't have room to put all your shoes in a shoe rack, store the pairs you wear less or that aren't in season in shoe boxes with a photo of the shoes taped to the box. You'll never have to go hunting through boxes again.

- Organize shoes by shoe type, starting with boots and moving on to pumps, ballet slippers, sneakers, etc.

Jewelry

- Invest in a good-quality jewelry box, where all your accessories are organized and easily accessible. They are often quite pricey, but jewelry can totally transform an outfit.

- Purchase a few jewelry trees for hanging larger costume necklaces and bracelets.

WORK IT

To find a completely new wardrobe in your closet, you need to mix pieces you have never mixed before. If you feel overwhelmed, think of the stores you visited. Inventing a great outfit does not necessarily have to be complicated. It's as simple as a dress and accessories, or a top, a bottom, shoes, and accessories. Have fun layering, mixing colors, trying new shapes with belts, and so on. (continued)

Remember, mix and match beyond your comfort zone. Creating a new look can be as easy as changing the belt, adding a necklace, or pairing boots with fun tights. In this experiment, aim to get at least five new outfits. But I bet you'll find a lot more. Consider your lifestyle, and put a twist on your usual looks for routine day-to-day tasks like going to work and running errands. Here are a few suggestions to get you started.

Combine interesting and unexpected colors and prints.

Camel

- Pair w/ cheetah
- Pair w/ crimson red

Chocolate

- Pair w/ paprika (fierce reddish orange)
- Pair w/ lime
- Pair w/ Tiffany blue

Pink

- Pair w/ khaki
- Pair w/ kelly green

Black and white

- Pair w/ yellow

Lavender

- Pair w/ zebra
- Pair w/ navy

Navy

- Pair w/ orange
- Pair w/ yellow

Tweak items to update them or make them your own.

- *Blazers:* Change the buttons and remove the shoulder pads.
- *Skirts:* Take a hem out to elongate, or hem shorter. Hand stitch a cluster of patches, or pin a brooch on the center or corner of a flat-front waistband.
- *Dresses:* Add a belt and cinch at the waist.
- *Blouses:* Dye a new bright color.
- *Boxy suit jacket:* Nip the waist by wearing a belt over the jacket.
- *Pearl necklace:* Pile them on and add a brooch as pendant.
- *Boots:* Resole the bottoms and give a mean polish and conditioning treatment. Get knee boots tailored and taken in to fit your leg perfectly.
- *Basic pumps or flat thong sandals:* Add stylish shoe clips; even use a brooch or clip-on earrings.

Layer the unexpected.

- Cami under a blouse, under a tailored menswear blazer
- Pile on long chains and pendant necklaces of three different lengths
- Wool shorts over opaque tights with a stacked peep-toe heel

Attention, Bargain Babes

As you peruse your closet, you'll realize that some pieces make you feel like the Schizo Shopper with two personalities and four body types. Start to create reject piles. There's no need to hang on to pieces that don't suit you. You can make use of them in another way, by selling them to a consignment shop for some extra cash, letting your girlfriends sort through the piles for themselves, or donating them to your local Goodwill and getting that warm and fuzzy feeling (not to mention a tax deduction). I know it can be hard to part with your fashion family, but sometimes love is best from a distance. Take a deep breath and begin to make room for future fashion friends.

Caring for Your Clothes

Every fashionista knows the importance of preserving her clothes. Looks cycle in and out of vogue, so your neon miniskirt from the eighties has a good chance of coming back in style one day. If you are going to invest serious cash in a beautiful cashmere-blend suit or a top designer dress, you want it to last. Giving yourself a closet make-over will go a long way to maintaining the integrity of your garments. Cramming everything into a tight space can ruin the shape of delicate clothes.

I also briefly discussed the importance of good hangers before, but let me elaborate. Different hangers do in fact place different stresses on the structure of the item they are supporting. Never hang delicates on a wire hanger, as it could distort the shape of the apparel and possibly damage the textile. Using foam or padded hangers ensures even weight distribution and helps stretching from slippage. Additionally, suits and jackets should always be placed on shouldered hangers. And always fold knits to retain shape, instead of hanging.

Shoes and bags can last a lifetime, or two, or three, if you treat them well and heal the daily wear and tear. Part of that is preserving their shape as they rest their little bodies in the closet. Stuff the insides of bags with tissue paper or a filler to keep the shape, and shoe trees or tissue paper for shoes. Do this especially after a day of sloshing through rain puddles to retain their shape and absorb moisture. Store your bags and shoes in their original cloth dust bags or in ventilated clear plastic stackable boxes from

The Container Store. A good stain guard treatment before debuting your purchase never hurt a fab pair of Louboutins or Ferragamos either. And don't be afraid to get shoes resoled or a heel reinforced to keep their legacy going on for years and years. Long live the power accessories!

Attention, Bargain Babes

If you are like me, you have well more than a few pair of shoes that are drop dead gorgeous, but literally kill your feet when you wear them. Well girls, our prayers have been answered. NYC shoe doctor Bob Schwartz can make your stilettos feel like sneakers. He is a godsend.

Where: 470 Park Avenue

Tel.: (800) ENE-SLOW

Website: www.eneslow.com

Those are the basics of good wardrobe maintenance. But there is a whole army of experts out there who can keep your cashmere as soft as a kitten's belly and your shoes as shiny as a marine's. Stylists and editors know whom to turn to when they want to repair the hardware on their coveted Birkin bag or get a stain out of a silk Chloé top. Let's hear from a few mavens on the best way to care for your clothes.

CARING FOR YOUR SWIMSUITS **with swimwear designer Lisa Letarte Cabrinha**

What makes a swimsuit a quality piece?

An amazing attention to fit and a soft, good-quality fabric are essential to a swimsuit's being a quality piece. A quality swimsuit will hug the skin perfectly and will almost mold to the body.

Are there any specifics shoppers should look for when buying swimwear?

The most important thing is the quality of the fabric—you want something that is going to hold up and stay looking new for a long time. Stay away from anything that is scratchy. Always inspect the stitching and any hardware or trims that are on the suit to make sure nothing is coming undone.

What is the best way to preserve a costly swimsuit?

Hand wash in Woolite and cold water. Never use bleach, and let it hang dry. To get sand out, run it under water and pull the fabric away from the liner—the sand should fall out. To help preserve the suit, rinse it out in fresh water after each use. Don't leave it in a hot car or out in the hot sun—this will damage the elastic and will also fade the color of your suit.

How long should swimsuits last?

It really depends on how often you wear your suits and how hard you are on them. If you surf every day, your suit is going to last probably only one season. For the normal beachgoer who has a couple of rotating suits in her wardrobe—she can get many summers out of her swimwear with proper care.

CARING FOR YOUR CASHMERE **with a representative from the Italian cashmere line Ballantyne, whose clients include Oprah Winfrey, Keira Knightley, and Nicole Kidman**

What is the simplest way to care for cashmere?

Wash it by hand with a gentle soap [WhiteandWarren .com has a great cashmere wash, and if you are in a pickle, you can always use a gentle baby shampoo]. Instead of wringing out the water, place it on a towel, and roll out the excess water. Shape it and lay flat to dry.

Why do cashmere sweaters get those funny little balls on them?

This is called pilling, a typical cashmere phenomenon. Pilling can happen when the cashmere is rubbed against something. It commonly occurs under sleeves that rub against the body, or on the front of sweaters where jackets and purses rub against the material. Most people assume pilling occurs over time, but this is generally not the case. The softer the sweater, the more likely it will pill. Also the shorter the fibers are, the more likely it will pill. (To remove pilling, you can purchase a de-piller from StacksandStacks.com, or gently use a razor to remove the pills. Be very careful, because you can create a hole.)

What causes those little holes that cashmere sweaters and socks get?

Moths can cause holes, as well as wear and tear. You can protect your cashmere from moths by using cedar balls or cedar wood drawers. Lavender sachets are another smell-good solution. You can always get holes stitched up.

Where is the best cashmere manufactured?

Scotland! Real cashmere is obtained from the goat's fine fleecy undercoat (also called the duvet), which is externally covered by thick, stiff hairs called "guard hair."

China is the world's largest producer of raw cashmere of the best quality.

CARING FOR YOUR BAGS, BELTS, SHOES, AND WALLETS **with Shoe Service Plus, one of New York City's premiere leather goods repair shops**

What are the top three ways to preserve the life of your leather goods?

Use shoe and handbag dust bags, utilize cleaning products, and go to a shoe repair shop for cleaning and repairs.

What are the most common repairs that people come in for?

Resoling the backs of shoes. Cleaning the handles or replacing the lining of bags.

What if the boot no longer fits around the leg, can you do anything to fix that?

If you would like to stretch the leg, it takes three to four days to put it in the machine. We can also add leather to the leg, but it will be more expensive.

Can you remove stains from leather and suede?

Yes, we can remove stains from leather and suede. However, stains on light-colored patent leather cannot be removed.

FASHION FIRST-AID KIT

There are flares for accidents on the road. Well, you need relief and rescue from fashion accidents too. Create your own little fashion first-aid kit filled with remedies for any debacle. Keep it in your car, your desk, at home, or all of the above.

Emergency: A white-chalky-streak-on-your-black-dress crisis
Store solution: Gal Pal garment deodorant pads
Home remedy: Briskly rub the freshly stained deodorant part of the dress against another part of the dry garment and voilà, the stain disappears.

Emergency: The cat just gave you a fur bath and you look like Garfield's twin.
Store solution: Gal Pal lint-remover mitts
Home remedy: Wrap masking tape around your hand like a boxer would do and pat your lint away.

Emergency: Your blouse seems to want to flash everyone your goodies, or a hem falls out of place while you are about to run out of the house.
Store solution: Topstick toupee tape
Home remedy: Strong double-sided tape

(continued)

Emergency: You spill a little gazpacho on your skirt.

Store solution: Tide-to-Go stick (Kelly Ripa's fave)

Home remedy: Laundry stain-remover sheets or a little seltzer water works wonders.

Emergency: The heels of your feet really hurt in those killer stilettos.

Store solution: Foot Petals Tip Toes and Killer Kushionz

Home remedy: Layered Band-Aids

DIY Recipes for Instant Style

It's time to cast your fears of crafts aside. Doing It Yourself (or, as I like to call it, Designing It Yourself) is a classic trend. There are stylish, inexpensive projects available for all levels that look practically identical to what you love in the stores. Some DIY projects are as simple as adding a crystal or a button onto a garment, and some more difficult ones require sewing machines and cutting. No matter what the level, DIY projects are great for parties or casual weekend get-togethers.

If your project does not come out as you envisioned the

first few times, don't be discouraged. DIYing can be like cooking: Sometimes the best outcomes stem from mistakes. Always maintain your style integrity and don't force yourself to wear something just because you spent a few hours sewing ribbon onto it. But don't stop trying and exploring.

DIYing allows you to take your personal style a step further by customizing clothing with added elements. So get those glue guns ready!

DIY UTENSILS

In order to get crafty, you'll need a little DIY kit handy in the house. Having it accessible is great for when you get the urge to change up a look but can't put anything more on the AmEx. Whip out your kit and create an entirely new item! Every kit varies depending on the person, but these basics are a good start.

- **Industrial-strength glue:** Great for gluing anything metal or plastic, try Permabond 102 or Gorilla Glue.
- **Hot glue and glue gun:** For fabrics and softer items.
- **Velcro:** Perfect for when you are in a super rush and don't have time to attach something with needle and thread.

- **Needle and thread:** Keep handy for a quick fix of a hem or a button.
- **Sharp scissors:** Try to use this pair only for your notions. Refrain from using on paper, since this will dull them faster.
- **Tape measure:** Small and easy to use, not industrial strength
- **Fine tweezers:** For picking up little beads and crystals

DIY INGREDIENTS LIST

Now for the yummy stuff.

- **Patches:** You can find these in packs or individually. Even better, take off patches from another jacket or item and recycle.
- **Crystals and stones:** I love the divine high shine of Swarovski crystals, but there are tons of additional great options that cost less.
- **Buttons:** They are available in a rainbow of colors, shapes, and fun textures. Hunt for great vintage buttons at flea markets to bring originality to a tired piece.
- **Beads:** These are great for creating detail on a garment or making jewelry.

- **Ribbon:** Satin, printed, velvet, and more. You can use ribbons for making anything from hair accessories to a belt.

- **Trim:** Textured lace, eyelet, fringe—trim design options are endless and can really add personality to accessories and clothes.

- **Buckles:** These are for more than just belts. Add them to bags, straps, and more.

- **Silk flowers:** From cool pins to beach flip-flops, they bring such happiness to any item.

Attention, Bargain Babes

Who doesn't love a great inexpensive item? We have all seen the awesome sweater in Target, or those really nice-looking jeans in Express, and thought, *Wow, only forty bucks. I have to have it.* Well, great minds think alike, because soon every other girl in your town, and the world, has the same item. Don't despair. You can have a little DIY moment and make your garment look completely different. No one will ever realize that you actually got it from the same place! A simple change of the buttons to a more bold statement button can be enough. Or try an embroidered patch on the pocket of a blazer.

EIGHT WAYS TO UPDATE A CARDIGAN

1. **Belt it:** Over the cardigan, use a grosgrain preppy belt, a wide patent belt, or a belt with a smashing buckle.

2. **Button up:** Change the original buttons to unique ones made of diamante pavé crystals or a great, painted vintage find.

3. **Go wild:** Add a rocker chain and cluster of studs on the wrists.

4. **Go romantic:** Add lace trim on the hem.

5. **Go rock star:** Stud the neckline with rivets or metal studs.

6. **Go glamazon:** Add a fur collar.

7. **Go tooty-fruity:** Add a cherry ornament or a patch on a pink cardigan.

8. **Go glitz:** Add a faux necklace to the neckline for a two-in-one sweater necklace effect.

DIY STYLE RECIPES

Here are some really cheap and chic DIY projects from some of the industry's top experts who know how to get their craft on. Cooking with these style chefs is as simple as boiling water. But the outcome is as sweet as a pecan pie. You can find most of the resources you need for the recipes below at your local crafts store or at mass chains like Michael's.

Daisy's Perfect Flower Pin

Go classic Carrie Bradshaw with a big flower on your chest if you want to bring spring style to a dreary day. Flowers make everyone smile, plus they're great for covering up noticeable stains or holes.

INGREDIENTS

- Oversize silk flower (can also use fake flowers in other materials)
- Gorilla Glue (or any other glue that works with metal and plastic—hot glue will not hold up long once it dries)
- Pinking shears or scissors
- Felt or fabric
- Pins with flat backs (Darice nickel-plated pins work well)

RECIPE

1. Cut the stem of the flower off, just at the base of the bottom of the flower.
2. Cut out a circle of the felt or fabric, about the size of a silver dollar.

3. Glue the felt or fabric onto the bottom of the flower, where you cut the stem off.
4. Glue the pin onto the back of the felt.
5. Turn upside down, petal side facing down, and let air dry in a cool place for about an hour.
6. Can be worn on a sheath dress, ribbon belt, purse, coat, or wherever you like.

Daisy's Chandelier Cardi

This is a terrific project to use all the beads you purchased in bulk at a blowout sale as you turn your favorite cardigan into a dazzling item. Try monochromatic black beads on a black cardigan, or metallic gray or silver beads on a gray sweater. Whether you go bold or playful, you are destined to shine.

INGREDIENTS

- Flat-knit cardigan
- Sparkly notions (large beads with a flat bottom, paillettes, or sequins with small holes inset for threading)
- Needle and thread (color similar to notion)
- Tailor's chalk

RECIPE

1. Lay sweater out flat on hard surface.
2. With the tailor's chalk, mark a creative pattern on the neckline and below where the beads will be sewn.
3. Attach beads securely on each mark on the sweater.
4. Shimmer and shine on with your new chandelier cardigan.

Daisy's Sweet and Simple Swimsuit

This one is brilliant if you have tons of bathing suit separates in solid colors that fit you well but lack a little oomph. For nice, inexpensive suits in every color to use for this project, try NewportNews.com or American Apparel.com. This is also a great way to spruce up your kid's swimsuits when you don't want to buy another swimsuit for her busy social calendar of swim play dates.

INGREDIENTS

- Solid-colored swimsuit (can be a one-piece, tankini, or two-piece)
- Flat decorative patch (I like to use bright-colored fruit like pineapples or strawberries, but you can choose the patch that suits your personality)

- Needle and thread (use a color closest to the patch)
- Double-sided tape

RECIPE

1. Thread needle and set aside (make sure to set it somewhere visible, like on a pin cushion).
2. Try on your swimsuit.
3. Test out where you want to place your patch by taping it on your swimsuit. Try placing in visible areas like near your neckline or near the waistband.
4. Mark the area with tailor's chalk.
5. Remove the swimsuit and lay it on a flat hard surface.
6. Stitch the patch securely onto the swimsuit.
7. You instantly have a new bathing suit!

Wouri Vice's Monogrammed Polos and Pullovers

Wouri, who has styled Hollywood's most dapper dudes and darlings, including Chris Rock, Diane Neal, Queen Latifah, and Alicia Keys, shares the best way to feel like a total prepster headed to your beach house in the Hamptons. Think Ralph Lauren or Palm Beach. A secret from Wouri: He loves to find high-end cashmere for less at Syms.

INGREDIENTS

- Basic polo shirt (go down a size to have a nice tailored fit)
- Basic knit pieces

RECIPE

1. Head to your local monogram shop and request that your initials be monogrammed over the left side of the top of the sweater, or on the polo shirt close to your heart. Choose a script that suits your personal style best. Choose contrasting or identical colors to the sweater or shirt for the embroidery thread. Nothing looks fresher than a crisp pair of white jeans and a monogrammed polo.

Note: Don't have a monogram shop in town? If you haven't noticed any monogram shops around, you can also ask your local tailor and seamstress if they offer monogramming. Also try local swap meets that supply gear to sports teams. They usually have a monogram machine.

Joyann King's Trench Coat Dress

Joyann, who has contributed to InStyle.com, Elle.com, Self.com, and Shopbop.com, offers a fresh update on America's favorite classic. This is a smart fix if you have a stain on the sleeve of your favorite trench that just won't come out.

INGREDIENTS

- Khaki classic trench coat (either short or long will work; if you do not have an old trench coat, Old Navy and Gap make great, affordable styles)
- Seam ripper
- Pinking shears
- Regular sewing scissors
- One yard of three- to four-inch leather strips or silk ribbon in your favorite color

RECIPE

1. Remove sleeves: Turn the jacket inside out and use the seam ripper to rip out the seam where the shoulders and sleeves attach. Clean up loose threads with the scissors. If sleeveless is not your style, another option is to cut the sleeves off at your mid to upper

arm and roll them a half-inch twice for a short-sleeve dress.

2. Shorten the dress to desired length. I recommend midthigh for a fashion-forward look. Use pinking shears to cut. These will keep the bottom from unraveling. If you want to spend an extra five dollars, you can have your local tailor hem it for a more finished look.

3. Belt it. Use leather strips or ribbon and wrap around your waist in an obi style (the middle of the fabric should start in front at your waist, then wrap around the back and knot again in the front). After you knot it, cut off the excess ribbon or leather five to six inches from the knot. While I prefer black, feel free to experiment with other colors here—hot pink, navy, red—all will look chic and give your dress more versatility.

Kirk Shannon-Butts's Big Kid Candy Necklace

A fashion editor for *Glamour* and an independent filmmaker, Kirk's got a tasty way to spruce up your weekend jeans and T-shirt look.

INGREDIENTS

- 1-inch-wide satin ribbon
- Round beads the size and look of medium and over-size gumballs. Make sure to get beads with two holes, one on each side. Four of each will do. Candy-like shades are preferred, such as sorbet hues or bold Crayola colors.
- Straight pin

RECIPE

1. Measure the ribbon around your neck, and cut about five additional inches of the length that falls just below your décolleté. The extra will be for tying a bow to secure the necklace.
2. Take the straight pin and stick it through the ribbon.
3. Stick the pin with the ribbon on it through the medium bead.
4. Do the same for each bead, rotating: medium, over-size, medium, oversize.
5. Once all eight beads are strung, try it on and tie a ribbon in the back to secure it.

6. You can get creative and use different shapes and colors of beads, like flat discs, then round beads, then flat discs.
7. It will look so pretty, you will want to eat it.

Julee Wilson's Really Simple Headband

As *RealSimple* Magazine's fashion editor, Julee, is always cooking up new ideas. She achieves her signature day-to-night look instantly with a cool and one-of-a-kind headband. It's also a chic way to tame flyaways. Head to Target for headbands and vintage stores for the brooch.

INGREDIENTS

- Half-inch-thick Goody elastic headband
- Brooch, either vintage or new

RECIPE

1. Apply headband on head.
2. Pin brooch so it lines up with the corner of your eye.
3. Change up pin based on your look and mood.

Veronica Webb's in the Name of Love Bracelets

Veronica's a supermodel and supermommy, who uses this project to bond with her kids when they are bored out of their minds. Shop for the kyanite blue glass beads at KyaniteGems.com and at FireMountainGems.com for wood and turquoise beads and crystals.

INGREDIENTS

- .5-mm diameter Stretch Magic Elastic
- Blue glass kyanite beads or turquoise or wooden beads
- Gold icon of your choice (think hearts or child's initials)
- Swarovski crystal 3-mm beads
- Big-eye beading needle

RECIPE

1. Measure off the circumference of your wrist with the elastic thread, leaving one inch extra for the knot at the end.

2. Tape one end to a dinner plate (so the beads don't slide off one end when you measure or test your bracelet).

3. Start adding beads to the thread (I like the rhythm of threes, so I string three kyanite beads, or turquoise

or wooden ones, and add a Swarovski crystal as a spacer after every third bead).

4. Add the charm to the center position of the bracelet.

5. When you give the bracelet to someone you love as a gift, write a lovely blessing or a wish. When they wear the bracelet, they will be reminded of your wish to them.

★ Bargain Babe Badge of Honor ★

I hope you have enjoyed the journey through all of shopping's greatest challenges and are now feeling the thrill of victory. You can stomp out fashion myths in your new Balenciaga boots that you scored by style stalking, befriending a sales girl, and showing patience while waiting for them to get marked down to a price that suited you. Vow to never say *I wish I could wear* or *I wish I could afford* again. Your new vocabulary consists of *Hmm, let me see what chapter applies to my little obstacle.* Do you need to sell a few pairs of shoes that you haven't worn in a while to get one great socialite pair of boots that will work for your entire fall wardrobe? Or maybe an easy switch of a few buttons on your blazer will instantly give your wardrobe a much-needed update. Long gone are the days of being stuck with an impulse buy because, though it was hot on Jennifer Aniston, it doesn't look the same on you. Celebrities are now going to be inspired by you! Saving and being stylish looks great on you.

Whenever you jump on the fashion Volkswagen, know that it is simply never too late. So this, my lovelies, is for you: the girl about town in a trendy area of NYC or the one in a small town in Georgia who dares to dream. I hope you are as inspired by my story as I am by yours.

Utilizing your new skills will be like living in a never-ending buy-one-get-one-free sale. Maybe you are getting extra cash savings, a coupon for a free tote bag, or a free session with a local style expert at a swanky boutique. For every gal who now feels empowered to shop with an editor's eye and no longer feels pressure to buy anything she doesn't like, I lift my platforms and say cheers to you. Step up to the Shoppers Throne. Aquamarine, amethyst, diamonds, pink tourmaline, it's all up to you. Choose your gem of choice as your Fashion Fairy Godmother officially crowns you a true and well-deserving Bargain Babe.

Style Glossary

armage: Also known as smash arm, a Daisy term that refers to the condition of standing or posing for a picture with your arms alongside your body, causing arms to look larger and fuller. The easy solution to armage is simply perching up or pivoting your elbows and placing hands on those hips.

Balenciaga: Pronounced "bah-lyn-see-yah-gah." Known for their IT bags and killer shoes.

beyond: An emotion and expression shared when something is amazingly terrific, sometimes so gratifying that you feel overwhelmed, in a fashionable, silly kind of way.

Burberry: Pronounced "burr-buh-ree." Known for their classic timeless trench and signature khaki, as well as their red and black tartan print.

cashmere: Made from the hair of the cashmere goat, this is one of the warmest, softest wools. There are many grades of cashmere available on the market now, with the finest made from the beard of the goat.

cheapie: An item that is not well made despite the label or cost.

Christian Louboutins: Pronounced "loo-booo-tuhn." The drop-dead gorgeous shoe line is referred to as Louboutins worldwide. Named after the Frenchman Christian Louboutin, the first to introduce the signature red sole on his often 5-inch heels and platforms.

cotton: The fabric has great durability and is ideal for a T-shirt or summer dress. Just make sure it feels good against the skin and has excellent resilience.

consignment: Selling or buying a slightly used item at a fraction of the retail cost.

D-ring: Metal piece of hardware in the shape of a D, used on bags, shoes, and luggage at the end of a leather or fabric strap.

DIY: Design it yourself, or do it yourself, a money-saving phenomenon that taps into your inner talents for creating at-home projects in fashion and beauty.

dolman sleeve: A fabulous sleeve that is exaggerated in

width and often length. Legends like Diana Ross, Cher, and Beyoncé have been known to wear this type of sleeve on dresses and tunics during performances. It is also a great way to hide excess arm bulge.

editor's eye: The shopping intensity and expertise level of a fashion professional, such as an editor or stylist. That means being able to spot pieces with style potential in a variety of settings and stores. It's attainable and achievable for all who do their homework.

fantastics: A group of people who are just that, fantastic. They can include absolutely anyone that you select, from a personal group of friends to a team of style gurus whom you admire.

Giuseppe Zanotti: Pronounced "jyuh-cep-ee zyah-naw-tey." A shoe designer known for exquisitely embellished statement shoes, loved by celebrities and rock stars like Beyoncé.

grosgrain: Popular silk or synthetic material often used for belts, in colors and patterns with vertical stripes.

jersey: A stylist favorite, a good-quality jersey will swing and flow with your walk and not droop and sag. The classic DVF wrap dress is constructed from matte jersey, one of the most flattering fabrics a girl can wear.

knits: When thread or yarn are looped either by hand or machine, it produces a knit fabric. High-end knits will feel smooth and will resist pilling (forming little balls) longer than lower-quality knits. Finer knits are delicate and can tear and snag very easily.

knockoff: An item, often in the clothing and accessories industry, that is designed to look like an original designer item and sold for a fraction of the cost. New York's Canal Street is a legendary district for selling designer knockoffs. The practice is illegal.

lace: A very delicate, ornamental fabric that can be extremely costly to produce, especially when made by hand. Beware of rough, scratchy varieties on cheaper garments.

leather and suede: Cheap skins often have a strong smell, while more expensive ones do not. When these skins are high quality, they are extremely soft and smooth.

linen: A natural fabric that should have a smooth surface and not be scratchy. Linen wrinkles easily, but the wrinkles should fall out once you've hung up the garment.

Lycra: This synthetic fabric changed the way clothes fit women of all shapes and sizes because of the stretch and flexibility it adds to any garment. It is particularly great for slimming undergarments.

market: A particular area of expertise or goods. An editor may cover a specific market, such as the accessories market, or shop the market for hot pink patent leather pumps.

matchy-matchy: A term that refers to when someone's outfit perfectly matches in color, print, designer, or any other element. This is not the same as monochromatic, which refers to one neutral color worn head to toe, like all white, or all black. Matchy-matchy isn't exactly a compliment.

muse: A designer's or creator's inspiration for their collection or company. This person can inspire products for the home, beauty, or fashion. They are often known for their individual style as well as beauty. Filmmaker Sofia Coppola has been one of Marc Jacobs's most famous muses.

notion: A sewing accessory such as a crystal or sequin that is applied to a garment or fashion accessory for added style.

"over it": A term to describe when a person no longer has the desire to wear, taste, or experience something. You can be over wearing a fad or over eating a fad food like cupcakes.

paillettes: Oversize flat sequins

polyester: A retro synthetic fabric that's been modernized, it performs surprisingly well in garment construction when of a particular grade.

rivet: A notion used for style and function on bags and shoes, often in brass or metal, resembling a stud.

satin: Although it wrinkles very easily, satin is a gorgeous fabric that is often used for cocktail, wedding, and other festive gowns.

sample sale: A sale that includes past samples from a designer's collection. An untraditional sample sale offers excess pieces in a variety of sizes and colors. Sample sales vary and can include press sample sales, private, invite only, online, and public sample sales. The items are always nonreturnable.

sample size: A specific size that a shoe or piece of clothing is produced in. Shoe sample sizes are usually a nine, and clothing is usually a two or four. Samples are used for the purpose of runway shows, photo shoots, and campaign ads.

silk: An expensive fabric made from silkworms. There are great imitation silks, such as viscose, that appear very similar but are less expensive.

stretch: Stretch fabrics will stretch in all four directions, unlike nonstretch fabrics that most likely stretch only two ways, lengthwise or crosswise. High-quality stretch fabrics should have great flexibility and resilience and not lose their shape quickly.

toe cleavage: The cracks of your toes that are visible on a shoe cut low near the toe area.

velvet: Formerly considered a luxury fabric, the woven fabric that is closely sheared to produce that smooth buttery feel is now available in everything from silk to cotton. Beware of cheap, bulky-looking velvets. High-quality velvet should be structured, smooth, and have a nice weight.

VPL: Visible panty lines, often caused by too-tight or ill-fitting undies. Occasionally a thong can be the culprit. This is a major fashion no-no.

VBL: Visible bra lines, often caused by bras that are too small in cup size and/or worn on the hook that causes a bit of back bulge.

warehouse sale: A massive sale of a designer or combination of designers featuring back stock, previous samples, and a variety of sizes and colors.

Appendix

Here are some of my favorite places, websites, and secret hideaways to shop for major deals on everything. Take this guide with you when shopping in any of the cities listed. Be sure to give these places a jingle in advance or check the website to make sure all the information is still the same. I'm not only looking to save you money in retail, I want you to save on gas too!

ATLANTA

BROAD STREET ANTIQUE MALL

The deal: all sorts of antique treasures
Where: 3550 Broad Street #F
Tel.: (770) 458-6316
Website: broadstreetantiquemall.com

THE CLOTHING WAREHOUSE

The deal: one of several chains in the southeastern states for classic vintage at its finest

Where: 420 Moreland Avenue N.E.

Tel.: (404) 524-5070

Website: theclothingwarehouse.com

STEFAN'S VINTAGE CLOTHING

The deal: In one of the oldest vintage boutiques in Atlanta, find everything from party dresses to fur stoles from eras older than your mom's birth year.

Where: 1160 Euclid Avenue N.E.

Tel.: (404) 688-4929

Website: stefansvintageclothing.com

AUSTIN

FEATHERS BOUTIQUE

The deal: well edited, neatly stocked, and well priced

Where: 1700B S. Congress Avenue

Tel.: (512) 912-9779

CHICAGO

DELICIOUSLY VINTAGE

The deal: Indulge in vintage delights galore while in the Windy City.

Where: 1747 S. Halstead

Tel.: (312) 733-0407

Website: dvchicago.com

LULU'S AT THE BELLE KAY

The deal: a fave with locals like Nate Berkus for everything from accessories to dresses

Where: 3862 N. Lincoln

Tel.: (773) 404-5858

Website: lulusbellekay.com

UNA MAE'S FREAK BOUTIQUE

The deal: a perfect mix of high- and low-end, vintage and new designers

Where: 1422 N. Milwaukee

Tel.: (773) 276-7002

Website: users.ren.com/unamae/www.unamaes.com

LOS ANGELES

DECADES/DECADES TWO

The deal: sister stores with vintage couture and designer consignment from Chanel, Gucci, Prada, and many other big labels

Where: 8214 Melrose Avenue

Tel.: (323) 655-0223; (323) 655-1960

Website: decadesinc.com

RESURRECTION

The deal: vintage designer items in the heart of one of L.A.'s most in-demand shopping locations

Where: 8006 Melrose Avenue

Tel.: (323) 651-5516

Website: resurrectionvintage.com

SHAREEN VINTAGE

The deal: great for something to wear to a movie premiere or a weekend date

Where: 350 N. Avenue 21

Tel.: (323) 276-6226

Website: shareenvintage.com

THE WAY WE WORE

The deal: a crash course on vintage in the fashion industry

Where: 334 S. LaBrea Avenue

Tel: (323) 937-0878

Website: thewaywewore.com

MELROSE FAIRFAX FLEA MARKET

The deal: shop over two hundred vendors on Sundays, and a portion of the proceeds go to a local high school

Where: 7850 Melrose Avenue

Tel: (323) 655-7679

Website: melrosetradingpost.org

ROSE BOWL FLEA MARKET

The deal: open Sundays until 4:30 p.m. with VIP admission available from 5:00 to 7:00 a.m. for those who want first dibs

Where: 1001 Rose Bowl Drive, Pasadena

Tel: (626) 577-3100

Website: rgcshows.com

MARKET STREET DISTRICT

The deal: find trendy colorful dresses for under six dollars and suits for under sixty dollars

Where: corner of Manchester Boulevard and Market Street, Inglewood 90301

Website: cityofinglewood.org

SANTEE ALLEY

The deal: Put on your walking shoes to search the alley for dresses, hoop earrings in bulk, and many other wholesale items.

Where: between Santee and Maple Avenues at East Twelfth Street, downtown

Website: fashiondistrict.org/show.aspx?mi=4698

LONDON

PORTOBELLO

The deal: one of London's largest antiques markets, open every Saturday from 5:30 a.m. to 5:00 p.m.

Where: Portobello Road and Westbourne Grove

Website: portobelloroad.co.uk

NEW YORK CITY

BEACON'S CLOSET

The deal: sell and shop in this Brooklyn landmark for urban hipsters

Where: 92 Fifth Avenue, Park Slope

Tel.: (718) 230-1630

Website: beaconscloset.com

FISCH FOR THE HIP

The deal: consignment designer digs from the likes of Phillip Lim and Marni

Where: 153 West 18th Street

Tel.: (212) 633-9053

Website: fischforthehip.com

HOOTI COUTURE

The deal: At one of Brooklyn's best vintage boutiques, not only are the clothes great, but the jewelry collection and home pieces are always well chosen.

Where: 321 Flatbush Avenue, Brooklyn

Tel.: (718) 857-1977

Website: hooticouture.com

INA

The deal: shop like NYC publicists and fashion editors at this haven for designer consignment

Where: 21 Prince Street #A, NoLita

Tel.: (212) 334-9048

151 Bleeker Street, NoHo

(212) 228-8511

101 Thompson Street, SoHo

(212) 941-4757

208 East 73rd Street, Uptown

(212) 249-0014

Website: inanyc.com

TOKYO JOE

The deal: Be patient as you search for treasures in the floor-to-ceiling racks.

Where: 334 East 11th Street

Tel.: (212) 473-0724

WHAT COMES AROUND GOES AROUND

The deal: known western wear and used Levis

Where: 351 West Broadway

Tel.: (212) 343-1225

Website: whatgoesaroundnyc.com

ZACHARY'S SMILE

The deal: Find one-of-a-kind duds from the likes of Tyra
Banks and *Glamour* magazine.

Where: 317 Lafayette Street

Tel.: (212) 965-8248

Website: zacharyssmile.com

BROOKLYN FLEA

The deal: scour over 150 vendors selling stylish goodies

Where: 176 Lafayette Avenue (Saturdays)

Brooklyn Bridge, 22 Water Street (Sundays)

Tel: (718) 935-1052

Website: brooklynflea.com

ANNEX ANTIQUE FAIR AND CHELSEA FLEA MARKET

The deal: hit all the bases at the Antique Market, Chelsea
Flea Market, and Hell's Kitchen Flea Market on Saturdays and Sundays

Where: West 39th Street between Ninth and Tenth Avenues

112 West 25th Street (between Sixth and Seventh Avenues)

West 25th Street between Broadway and Sixth Avenue

Tel.: (212) 243-5343

Website: hellskitchenfleamarket.com

New York City is the sample sale mecca. Here is a list of my favorites, which are often held in the spring. Check local sites like NYMag.com around February for daily updates on public sales.

AEFFE SAMPLE SALE

The deal: one of New York's best and longest-running sample sales at a showroom for Italian designers like Moschino, Jean Paul Gaultier, and Alberta Ferretti

When: annually in the spring

Tel.: (212) 632-9300

INTERMIX WAREHOUSE SALE

The deal: the who's who of fashion labels, including Nina Ricci, Sergio Rossi, and See by Chloé

When: February and November

Website: intermixonline.com

METROPOLITAN PAVILION

The deal: This venue holds sample and warehouse sales for Kate Spade, Jimmy Choo, Intermix, and Hermès. Sign up for the mailing list for updates on upcoming sales.

Where: 125 West 18th Street

Tel.: (212) 463-0200

Website: metropolitanevents.com

PRADA SAMPLE SALE

The deal: Prada and Miu Miu for men, women, and occasionally children

When: the spring and summer seasons

Website: pradasamplesale.com (active only during sale season, the site enables you to request an invite)

WHOLESALE FASHION DISTRICT

The deal: Buttons, zippers, hats, and ball gowns can be found in the fashion capital of the world.

Where: between 30th and 40th Streets, from Ninth Avenue to Broadway

Tel.: (212) 398-7943 (Fashion Center Information Kiosk)

Website: fashioncenter.com

MIAMI

C MADELEINE'S

The deal: The Attic offers lower prices than the rest of the store's vintage designer items, because of missing labels.

Where: 13702 Biscayne Boulevard

Tel.: (305) 945-7770

Website: shop.cmadeleines.com

SAN FRANCISCO

AMERICAN RAG CIE

The deal: an all-time classic store for denim, dresses, and
accessories

Where: 1305 Van Ness Avenue

Tel.: (415) 474-5214

Website: amrag.com

CRIS

The deal: a chic consignment boutique in Nob Hill

Where: 2056 Polk Street

Tel.: (415) 474-1191

LA ROSA VINTAGE

The deal: On historic Haight Street, love and fashion peace
reign supreme in this former hippie enclave.

Where: 1711 Haight Street

Tel.: (415) 668-3744

SEATTLE

RED LIGHT VINTAGE

The deal: known in Seattle as the solution to many style
 problems

Where: 4560 University Way NE

Tel.: (206) 545-4044

Website: redlightvintage.com

WASHINGTON, DC

ANNIE CREAMCHEESE

The deal: cute options that go way beyond the red, white,
 and blue color palette

Where: 3279 M Street NW

Tel.: (202) 298-5555

Website: anniecreamcheese.com

INGA'S ONCE IS NOT ENOUGH

The deal: known as the First Lady of resale couture

Where: 4830 MacArthur Boulevard NW

Tel.: (202) 337-3072

Website: ingafashiontherapist.com

MEEPS VINTAGE FASHIONETTE

The deal: Stylish college coeds and urban hipsters search two floors of vintage digs and designs.

Where: 2104 18th Street NW

Tel.: (202) 265-6546

Website: meepsdc.com

EASTERN MARKET

The deal: fresh food, crafts, and ethnic attire at this historic fair on Sundays

Where: 225 7th Street SE

Tel.: (703) 534-7612

Website: easternmarket.net

Websites

Don't worry if your city wasn't listed in the section above. You can still find amazing clothes no matter where you live, and from the comfort of your own home. These sites are useful resources for anyone—even if you are smack dab in the center of New York City.

- WhereTraveler.com
- Yelp.com
- LuckyMag.com
- DailyCandy.com
- Citysearch.com
- Metromix.com
- Splendora.com
- local bloggers
- local city paper

Major Shopping Outlets

Here are some top outlets that will fill your closet with all-American faves like Ralph and Calvin, as well as the likes of top French, Italian, and British designers such as Roberto Cavalli and Gucci. Check websites in advance for the outlet nearest you, or a great outlet close to your next getaway. Most are just a quick road trip away.

CHELSEA PREMIUM OUTLETS

The deal: A Balenciaga number, a divine Dior pick, or a star-worthy Roberto Cavalli—whatever designer you fancy, you can find it here at significantly less than the retail value.

Website: premiumoutlets.com

PRIME OUTLETS

The deal: Whether you are a Burberry Babe or a Coach Cutie, you'll be able to satisfy your style cravings.

Website: primeoutlets.com

TANGER OUTLETS

The deal: If you are thirsting for Juicy or loyal to First Lady Michelle Obama's favorite, J.Crew, this outlet is the way to go.

Website: tangeroutlet.com

Discount Stores

BURLINGTON COAT FACTORY

The deal: Although it's well-stocked with coats from Calvin Klein and Miss Sixty, it houses more than just warm-weather goods. The Baby Depot allows customers to register for everything the babe will need until it's time to graduate from preschool.

Website: burlingtoncoatfactory.com

CENTURY 21

The deal: Look on each floor for deals as much as 85 percent off retail prices.

Website: c21stores.com

DAFFY'S

The deal: a great selection of designer clothing for adults and kids

Website: daffys.com

DSW SHOE WAREHOUSE

The deal: Shop online from thousands of pairs of designer shoes and receive free returns 365 days of the year. Then check the purses section, if you still have energy.

Website: dsw.com

FILENE'S BASEMENT

The deal: Always good for designer sales, this discount stalwart is also infamous for amazing bridal sales.

Website: filenesbasement.com

LOEHMANN'S

The deal: Check select stores' Back Room for exclusive designer and couture items.

Website: loehmanns.com

MARSHALLS

The deal: Shoe fiends will love the amazing shoe section with over five hundred designers, while foodies can indulge in gourmet spices and marinades.

Website: marshallsonline.com

ROSS

The deal: great options for teens and college coeds, like Harajuku sneakers

Website: rossstores.com

SYMS

The deal: simply a classic discount store

Website: syms.com

T.J. MAXX

The deal: Ralph Lauren towels, Tommy Hilfiger comforters, and Coach footwear are just a few of the biggies in this top discount store. The chain's home stores boast lines like Le Creuset, and amazing furniture.

Website: tjmaxx.com

Department Stores

BARNEYS NEW YORK

Annual Sales: The store holds its famous Warehouse Sales in February and August.

Outlet: Barneys New York Outlet

Website: barneys.com

BERGDORF GOODMAN

Annual sales: post–Memorial Day world-famous designer shoe sale

Website: bergdorfgoodman.com

BLOOMINGDALE'S

Annual sales: Check out the Mad About Shoes promotion (typically at the end of May, mid-August, and mid-February), where you get $50 off when you spend

$200 to $299, $100 off when you spend $300 to $499, and $150 off when you spend $500 or more. But you have to use your Bloomingdale's card.

Website: bloomingdales.com

JCPENNEY

Website: www.jcpenney.com

KOHL'S

Website: kohls.com

MACY'S

The deal: Special 10 percent off and free shipping are provided to out-of-state shoppers. Call 800-316-6166 for the Travel Service Line.

Website: Macys.com

NEIMAN MARCUS

The deal: Every time you use your store credit card you automatically earn two "InCircle" points for every dollar you spend. You can redeem these points for, say, a flight (similar to airline rewards), a gift card, or general swag.

Website: www.neimanmarcus.com

Outlet: Last Call Store

Website: nmlastcallstore.com

NORDSTROM

Annual sales: The Nordstrom Anniversary Sale in July has become legendary among Nordstrom customers nationwide who enjoy outstanding savings on the most exciting new fall merchandise before the season starts.

Website: shop.nordstrom.com

Outlet: Nordstrom Rack

SAKS FIFTH AVENUE

Outlet: Off 5th

Website: saksfifthavenue.com

SEARS

The deal: Lands' End designs special in-house and green collections.

Website: sears.com

Designer Bridal Sales

There are ways to get top-quality gowns worth tons for well under retail. With all your savings, you will be able to put the extra money toward something that you can use for a much longer time. Try these bridal resources for extreme savings that will lead you into marital bliss.

BEST BRIDAL DEPARTMENT SALE: SAKS FIFTH AVENUE BRIDAL SALE

The deal: One of the top bridal salons, Saks carries designers like Amsale, Vera Wang, Monique Lhuillier, and Reem Acra. Open a Saks charge account and receive an extra discount!

When: Their annual bridal sample sale happens in select states during the first six months of the year. Check your local Saks or SaksFifthAvenue.com for exact dates.

Website: saksfifthavenue.com

BEST STAR GOWN SALE: KLEINFELD MANHATTAN

The deal: Women are known to fly from all over the country to shop the sample sales. Check to get dates on regular blowout sales and annual sample sales, happening several times a year.

Website: kleinfeldbridal.com

BEST DISCOUNT STORE BRIDAL SALE: FILENE'S BASEMENT

The deal: Take a team of friends and plan out a strategy for getting the most options to try on while fighting the crowd. Use your sample sale strategies and boost them with shots of espresso.

Website: filenesbasement.com

BEST WEBSITE FOR DESIGNER LOOKALIKES: MAGGIE SOTTERO

The deal: Princess gowns (most under a thousand dollars) that can compete with the industry's high-end designers.

Websites: maggiesottero.com and www.sotteroandmidgley.com

SOMETHING BORROWED OR SOMETHING NOT SO BLUE

The deal: Rent a designer dream dress to look like a million bucks and pay next to nothing.

Website: weddingdressmarket.com

NOT SO USED

The deal: Check these websites for brides selling the gowns they have worn for a whopping three hours.

Websites: eBay.com, www.craigslist.org, and www.budget bridalgowns.com

BEST CHAIN STORE BRIDAL GOWNS: J. CREW

The deal: Some of the prettiest gowns you will ever see for as cheap as three hundred dollars! They offer complimentary bridal shopping services and are a perfect resource for the bridesmaids and for accessories.

Website: jcrew.com

High-Fashion, Low-Cost Chain Stores

TRENDY PIECES INSPIRED DIRECTLY FROM THE RUNWAYS OF PARIS, MILAN, NYC, AND LONDON:

- Anthropologie
- Forever 21
- French Connection
- H&M
- Joyce Leslie
- Mandee
- Mango
- Rainbow
- Target
- Topshop
- UNIQLO
- Urban Outfitters
- Zara

CLASSICS AND ESSENTIALS:

- American Apparel
- Ann Taylor
- Club Monaco
- Express
- J.Crew

- The Limited
- Madewell
- Martin + Osa
- New York & Company
- Old Navy

SHOES, BAGS, AND ACCESSORIES:

- ALDO
- Bakers
- DSW Show Warehouse
- Nine West
- Steve Madden

Terrific Chain Thrift Stores

BUFFALO EXCHANGE

Website: buffaloexchange.com

COUNCIL THRIFT SHOPS

Website: ncjwla.org/council_thrift_shops/

GOODWILL

Website: goodwill.org

HOUSING WORKS

Website: housingworks.org

OUT OF THE CLOSET

Website: outofthecloset.org

SALVATION ARMY

Website: salvationarmyusa.org

Junior Stores and Brands

ALLOY CATALOG

Website: store.alloy.com

ALL THE RAGE

Website: alltherageonline.com

AMERICAN EAGLE

Website: ae.com

AMICLUBWEAR

Website: amiclubwear.com

AV MAX

Website: avmaxaccessories.com

BILLABONG

Website: billabong.com

CHARLOTTE RUSSE

Website: charlotterusse.com

CLAIRE'S

Website: claires.com

CUTESYGIRL

Website: cutesygirl.com

DELIAS

Website: store.delias.com

DOLLHOUSE

Website: dollhouse.com

FIRE LA

Website: firela.com

GIRLPROPS

Website: girlprops.com

GOJANE

Website: gojane.com

GRASS CLOTHING

Website: grassclothing.com

HURLEY

Website: Hurley.com

ICING

Website: icingbyclaires.com

JOHNNY MARTIN

Website: johnnymartinjuniors.com

JUNK FOOD

Website: junkfoodclothing.com

LULU'S

Website: lulus.com

NECESSARY OBJECTS

Website: necessaryobjects.com

RAMPAGE

Website: rampage.com

ROXY

Website: roxy.com

RUE21

Website: rue21.com

SOUNDGIRL

Website: soundgirl.com

UNIONBAY

Website: unionbay.com

WANTED

Website: wantedshoes.com

WET SEAL

Website: wetseal.com

Shopping Events

Round up the girls for a night or day of shopping multiple lines and designer discounts, all under one fashionable roof. Get pampered with goodie bags, entertainment, bites, and beverages, all while saving a lot off retail prices. The shopping event trend has taken over by storm, and you can find one in almost every state. Check the websites for particulars on when you need to pencil them into your schedule.

BILLION DOLLAR BABES

The deal: One of the first and best, BDB offers access to exclusive designers like Valentino and Chloe, in person and online.

Website: billiondollarbabes.com

DIVINE DESIGN

The deal: Rub shoulders and shopping bags with Hollywood's most fashionable while supporting Project Angel Food, a charity that provides daily meals for people homebound or disabled by HIV/AIDS and other serious illnesses.

Website: divinedesign.org

LUCKY SHOPS NYC

The deal: The experts of *Lucky* magazine use their editor's eye to select the most fashionable pieces from designers like Catherine Malandrino, Marc Jacobs, Rebecca Taylor, and Theory.

Website: luckyshops.com

SHECKY'S GIRLS NIGHT OUT

The deal: Practically the hottest fashion ticket in every town. Happening all throughout the year, find unique indie and never-before-seen designers.

Website: girlsnightout.sheckys.com

SUPER SATURDAY

The deal: The Rolls-Royce of garage sales, this annual Hamptons event is sponsored by Donna Karan and *In-Style* magazine. You'll have to fight celeb fans like Kelly Ripa and Elisabeth Hasselbeck for the bargain clothes.

Website: ocrf.org

DIY Resources

No matter if you are a DIY Diva or simply experimenting, try the favorite stores of *Project Runway* fashion designers and stylists for affordable and stylish fabrics, notions, trim, supplies, tools, and more. Check the websites for select online ordering, classes, the closest location near you, and exclusive discounts.

BEADING EMPORIUM

Website: the beading-emporium.com

BRITEX NOTIONS

Website: shopbritexnotions.com

DERSH FEATHER AND TRADING CORPORATION

Website: dershfeather.com

HOBBY LOBBY

Website: hobbylobby.com

JOANN'S FABRIC

Website: Joann.com

M&J TRIMMING

Website: mjtrim.com

MICHAELS

Website: michaels.com

MOOD FABRIC

Website: moodfabrics.com

MOTHER PLUCKER FEATHER COMPANY

Website: motherplucker.com

SOUTACHE EMBELLISHMENTS

Website: soutacheribbons.com

TOHO SHOJI

Website: tohoshoji-ny.com

UNITED BEADS, INC.

Website: unitedbeadsus.com

Bond with the TV Remote

Channel surf and shop top designer lines and boutique finds from the likes of Scoop, Iman, and Molly Simms at reasonably low prices and amazing payment plans.

- HSN
- QVC

Acknowledgments

Fashion has never been complicated for me. It has always been more like indulging in a Diet Coke when you've been strictly on a flat water fast—an instant rush. Writing this book was sharing my true calling: the search for shopping solutions. It is dedicated to the women of style whom I have encountered within my adventurous thirty years on this earth. They have shown me how to become who I desire to be with exactly what I have in my heart, soul, and personal checking account. It's more than finding a bargain. It's about discovering and embracing my personal loves and appreciating others' style. It's about taking risks and being fearless. It's about making my dreams a reality. Dressing well not only creates a great picture, it makes you feel like a new woman who can conquer the world.

I'm indebted to my family matriarchs like Granny and Nana. There is the never-ending list of stylish women in my family like my aunt Linda, who was the eighties toast of the town in white stiletto leather booties and mini-dresses. To my lovely parents, thank you for supporting my style addictions, fashion-crazed phases of endless must haves, and shopping trips to LA & NYC. Aunt Dee, Aunty Carolyn, Tammi, Penny, Mommy Joy, Aunt Lucy, Aunt Sandra, you sure have shown me what a woman of style and virtue is all about.

Thanks to the classmates who thought I was crazy in high school for wearing silk neckerchiefs, oversize patent leather bags, and mile-high platform shoes with my Catholic schoolgirl plaid uniform. Even then I knew all press is good press.

Super thanks to the most fashionable, amazing, driven school in the world, Howard University, where *Every day is a fashion show* was the unspoken motto whispering in the trees.

Sydne Bolden, you are my hero, and I will forever consider you my boss. Thank you for teaching me everything I know.

Suze, my Jewish godmother, your support, smile, and career guidance and advice are priceless. Thanks for teaching me the power of color.

To my fashionable besties Joelle, Kahlana, Love, Chimere, Tunisia, Brother, Jasaun, Erica, Jasmine, Weyni, Eric, and Karen, thank you for always being the stylish life of the party, coast to coast.

To Ro, I'm your biggest fan for more reasons than one (one including phone numbers written in lipstick). Thank you for your love. You are my everything.

Pastor, you were right: more prayer, more power.

Jennifer Bergstrom, Patrick Price, and the Gallery Books family rock like David Yurman cocktail rings, all night long, and until the effervescent break of dawn.

Dream Team Meg Thompson and Lisa Leshne, thank you for not only being amazing agents, but warm and fuzzy in-box fillers. You gals rule the school.

Larry Kirshbaum, you are a brilliant man.

Nancy and Rebecca, thank you for your patience and skills.

To my Hollywood icons and the White House role models. Although some may see them as distant, their existence has been extremely evident and personal, and has helped me evolve my style. Even if we haven't met, I feel like we are kindred spirits. I credit Beyoncé for fearlessly embracing voluminous, honey-hued tresses and helping women across the planet fall in love with the smallest part of all our bodies—the ribcage and waist. Diana Ross for giving me the desire to wear floor-length gowns, sequins, lamé, and plenty of sparkles and shine morning, noon, and night. Michelle Obama for putting her stamp of approval on some signature elements that I have been embracing for years, like color, belts, and the oh-so-lovely full skirt. Carrie Bradshaw, my very number one NYC best friend, for helping me to find both labels and love.

All of these ladies are so special, so different, but still very alike—taking quiet stand to be themselves. They went against the grain for what they loved and in turn made everyone obsessed.

Early on in my life, I discovered that the two best accessories are joy and confidence. And thanks to my life inspiration, I have never run dry on either.

Most important, I have to thank the magnificent, marvelous, wondrous, triumphant Heavenly Father. Without you God, there would be no me, no queen of effortless chic, no sequins-filled closets, no goats to make cashmere, oh wow that could be a nightmare. I thank you God, for life, love, and liberty.

About the Author

The self-described Queen of Effortless Chic, DAISY LEWELLYN has covered the fashion and accessories market for *InStyle, Glamour,* and *Essence* magazines and is a regularly featured style and beauty expert on major morning shows and national networks, including the Style Network, E!, and Fox. She is based out of Los Angeles and dibbles and dabbles in NYC as often as possible.